HANGING JUDGE

Isaac C. Parker, the Hanging Judge of the United States Court for the Indian Territory, 1875–96. (Courtesy Archives and Manuscripts Division of the Oklahoma Historical Society.)

HANGING JUDGE

By

Fred Harvey Harrington

Foreword by Larry D. Ball

<small>ILLUSTRATIONS FROM PHOTOGRAPHS</small>

University of Oklahoma Press
Norman and London

TO HOLLY,

who was born in the Judge Parker country

Library of Congress Cataloging-in-Publication Data

Harrington, Fred Harvey, 1912–
    Hanging judge / by Fred Harvey Harrington ; foreword by
Larry D. Ball
        p. cm.
    Originally published: Caldwell, Idaho; Caxton Printers, 1951.
    Includes bibliographical references and index.
    ISBN 0-8061-2839-9 (alk. paper)
    1. Parker, Isaac Charles, 1838–1896. 2. Judges—United
States—Biography.   3. United States. District Court (Arkansas :
Western District)   4. Criminal justice, Adminisration of—
Indian Territory—History—19th century.   I. Title.
KF368.P32H35   1996
347.73′14′092—dc20
[b]
[347.30714092]
[B]   95-42983
                                                              CIP

The paper in this book meets the guidelines for permanence and
durability of the Committee on Production Guidelines for Book
Longevity of the Council on Library Resources, Inc.♾

1   2   3   4   5   6   7   8   9   10

Table of Contents

TABLE OF CONTENTS

List of Illustrations

Foreword

Isaac C. Parker occupies a unique place in the frontier judicial tradition. As presiding judge of the U.S. District Court for the Western District of Arkansas for twenty-one years (1875–1896), he tried cases not only from his primary jurisdiction but also from Indian Territory (present-day Oklahoma). In 1834, many years before Parker assumed the bench, Congress had attached this region to the U.S. District Court in Arkansas, with its seat in Little Rock. When the national lawmakers divided this federal bench in 1851, they appended the Indian lands to the newly created Western District Court, headquartered in Van Buren, Arkansas. Twenty years later, the court relocated to nearby Fort Smith. One reason for this attachment was to obtain the Arkansans necessary to serve as jurors for cases arising in Indian Territory.

As a result of this somewhat awkward judicial arrangement, Indian Territory provided the U.S. District Court in Arkansas with an appreciable case load. Furthermore, after the Civil War, this remote land spawned an ever-increasing roster of problems. Indians living in Indian Territory resented the forcible relocation from their eastern homes, and now the federal government added to their displeasure by reducing the size of some reservations as punishment for having joined the Confederacy, and by resettling warlike Plains tribes in Indian Territory. While Indian courts were empowered to try many cases arising among the American Indians, the presence of such a wide array of mutually hostile Indian nations conspired to create an atmosphere of violence and distrust. Moreover, the entry of large numbers of whites in Indian Territory contributed much to the growing crime rate. Some of these intruders came legally, to work on the new railroads or with the growing cattle industry. Other Anglos, however, came in criminal fashion, as landgrabbers or as peripatetic desperadoes seeking sanctuary from the law.

Although writers often have exaggerated the amount of violence and mayhem in Indian Territory in the late nineteenth century, the problems were sufficiently alarming to the U.S. marshals in Fort Smith—the officials who made arrests for Judge Parker—to warrant the employment of a large corps of deputy marshals. By the time Parker assumed the federal bench in 1875, the incidence of lawless deeds had reached high proportion in this troubled appendage to the Western District Court.

In spite of a high degree of interest in the sanguinary details of Judge Parker's tenure at Fort Smith, this notable bench still lacks an up-to-date, comprehensive scholarly study. The voluminous records of the court are available in

National Archives repositories, but most interested writers have devoted their pens to largely superficial treatment of the more sensational aspects of Parker's career. Samuel W. Harman's *Hell on the Border: He Hanged Eighty-Eight Men* (1898; reprint University of Nebraska Press, 1992) is the most widely used reference. Encyclopedic in nature and very informative, Harman's facts should nevertheless be used very carefully. As Fred Harvey Harrington observes, Harman includes firsthand recollections but "overemphasizes the last third of Parker's years" as presiding judge and makes "many direct misstatements" (pp. 198–99). While Homer Croy's *He Hanged Them High: An Authentic Account of the Fanatical Judge Who Hanged Eighty-Eight Men* (New York: Duell, Sloan, and Pearce, 1952) is perhaps the most popular biographical account, it deals only with hangings and a few badmen. Glenn Shirley has written numerous books about various aspects of law enforcement and lawlessness in Indian Territory. He presents a well-researched and reliable account of the Parker era in *Law West of Fort Smith: A History of Frontier Justice in the Indian Territory, 1834–1896* (New York: Henry Holt, 1957). More recently, the University of Oklahoma Press has published a well-received study by Jeffrey Burton that illustrates how the federal government employed the U.S. Courts, including Judge Isaac Parker's bench, to reduce the autonomy of the Five Civilized Tribes and prepare the region for statehood (*Indian Territory and the United States, 1866–1906: Courts, Government, and the Movement for Oklahoma Statehood* [1995]).

Of the many books devoted to Isaac C. Parker, Fred Harvey Harrington's remains perhaps the most balanced and well-researched. *Hanging Judge* represents the work of a mature scholar. Born in 1912 in Watertown, New York, Harrington earned a B.A. degree at Cornell University and, in 1937, a Ph.D. at New York University. He then joined the Department of History at the University of Wisconsin, Madison, but three years later he became the chair of the Department of History at the University of Arkansas, Fayetteville. In 1944 Harrington returned to the University of Wisconsin, where he had a long and distinguished career in the Department of History and in various administrative positions, eventually serving as president of the university.

While Harrington's scholarly training and primary field of writing was in American diplomatic history, his brief stay in northwestern Arkansas was sufficient to introduce him to that region's most famous character, Judge Isaac C. Parker. In 1946 Harrington announced that he was at work on a book about this frontier jurist. ("Hanging Judge Parker: The Man and Not the Legend," *Arkansas Historical Quarterly* 5: 58–77.) He had progressed far enough to lament the unfortunate work of "the popularizers, the fiction writers, [and] the tellers of tall tales." "Isaac Parker needs no dressing up," declared Harrington, because "he was interesting and important in his own right." His prediction that Hollywood scriptwriters would eventually "present the matter in an even more distorted fashion" was even more prescient.

It is the good fortune of present-day readers that this fine scholar began his research in the 1940s, because he was able to interview not only James Parker, Isaac Parker's grandson, but also other persons who had known the popular judge. As the bibliographic essay in *Hanging Judge* reveals, Harrington performed an admirable degree of research, including work in the National Archives at Washington, D.C., and in libraries and historical societies throughout Arkansas and Oklahoma. Acquainted with the broad range of works of other scholars in American history, Harrington was able to avoid the excessive adulation that other authors had bestowed upon Parker. The historian also presented a more balanced and sympathetic treatment than did many popular writers of the Indians who faced the imperious judge.

Hanging Judge represents a significant step forward in writings about the U.S. District Court for the Western District of Arkansas and its most famous jurist. Although Harrington ignored the antebellum history of relations between the federal bench in Arkansas and the Indians to the west, he presented the most solid and perceptive account of Parker's tenure. Readers of *Hanging Judge* will note the skepticism with which he approaches the many outlaws of that unfortunate land, who are accorded heroic qualities by popular writers. "Robin Hood did not ride the Western plains," admonishes Harrington (p. 29). At times he cannot resist sprinkling bits of wit among such critical remarks. In noting that Belle Starr, the infamous female outlaw, was not "a lady Robin Hood," Harrington goes on to say that this "nymphomaniac" never led a band of outlaws. "Belle Starr slept with many outlaws," concluded the author, "but gave orders to very few" (pp. 90–91). Nor does he go out of his way to gloss over the boorish behavior of frontiersmen in general. Some, he rightly observes, were "foul-mouthed and poorly educated" (p. 83). In rather daring fashion for his day, Harrington discusses the crude and often brutal sexual practices that were revealed in testimony before Judge Parker (pp. 102–16).

Harrington obviously is taken with the imposing frontier jurist, but he attempts to be evenhanded. He appropriately corrects the misconception that Parker presided at eighty-eight hangings, indicating that the more accurate figure is probably seventy-nine. In spite of Parker's desire to make a public example of such vicious men, Harrington points out that after 1881, Parker followed the national trend restricting the viewing of executions to a few persons behind stockade walls. Murder cases were few when compared with the thousands of lesser crimes that the judge tried—bootlegging, gambling, and livestock theft, among others. In spite of his admiration for Parker, Harrington admits that the jurist frequently abused his position. Not only did he employ the power of the bench to sway juries, but he also made "loaded comments" about defendants and their attorneys (p. 134).

The point of much of his official duties, Parker believed, was to protect the Indians and to provide them with "a breathing spell" before the inevitable Anglo tide of settlers overran Indian Territory (p. 168). Even so, the Indians complained about the Fort Smith tribunal. They disliked the necessity of traveling great distances to the court, which (from their point of view) was in a foreign land. They objected to the rough-handed and often corrupt practices of the deputy U.S. marshals, as well as to the anti-Indian attitude of the Arkansans who served as jurors in Fort Smith. The jurisdiction of the Western District Court over Indian Territory came to end in 1896, however, when Congress authorized a new federal bench within the formerly attached region. On November 17 of that year, Isaac C. Parker died.

The decision of the University of Oklahoma Press to

issue a paperback edition of *Hanging Judge* is most welcome. In the absence of a new and up-to-date work synthesizing recent research on the Parker court and utilizing the additional archival materials now available, Fred Harvey Harrington's volume still stands as the most objective and perceptive work on the subject. His scholarly treatment of Isaac C. Parker and his court is meshed with a wit and charm that softens some of the more grisly aspects of his subject. It is unfortunate that the author was not able to see his volume in print once again. Fred Harvey Harrington died in April 1995, just a short time before *Hanging Judge* was scheduled to reappear. Nonetheless, readers will have a new opportunity to acquire an appreciation of his work. The University of Oklahoma Press is to be congratulated for restoring this volume to its rightful place in the library of frontier law enforcement.

Larry D. Ball

Arkansas State University
August 1995

Preface

Judge Parker ... tried and sentenced to death more murderers than any judge who ever sat within the limits of the United States.

—Philander C. Knox, Theodore
Roosevelt's Attorney General

This is a story of the American Southwest in the days after the Civil War.

The land now known as Oklahoma was then called the Indian Territory; and it was one of the last and wildest of the American frontiers.

It was a region noted for its famous outlaws. Here rode the Daltons and the Youngers. This was the Belle Starr country; headquarters for the Cook and Buck and Doolin gangs. It was the home of Ned Christie and Cherokee Bill, Henry Starr and Felix Griffin, Whisky Jack and Glory Bill and the Verdigris Kid.

Here, too, in the border city of Fort Smith, lived the outlaws' greatest enemy. He wore no guns and went afoot, but the bad men rated him as a formidable foe.

He was Isaac Charles Parker, the Hanging Judge of the United States Court for the Indian Territory.[1] For twenty-one years (1875-96) this judge fought the desperadoes of the Southwest, and in these two decades he sent nearly eighty killers to the gallows.

This is the story of the Hanging Judge and of the men who stood with him against the desperadoes, so that the Southwest might become a land where all could prosper and none need feel afraid.

Many old friends and new have helped me bring Judge Parker back to life. Professor D. Y. Thomas of the University of Arkansas encouraged me to go into this field. Professor Richard N. Current of the University of Illinois read the entire manuscript. Dean H. M. Hosford and Professor W. B. Mahan of Southern Methodist University have given me much assistance, as have Grant Foreman of Muskogee, Oklahoma; Clarence F. Byrns of the *Southwest American* (a Fort Smith newspaper); Judge J. M. Hill and J. B. McDonough, both of whom knew Parker; James Parker, the judge's grandson; Dean John Clark Jordan and Professor Dorsey D. Jones of the University of Arkansas; the Honorable John H. Miller, who holds Judge Parker's old job as Judge of the United States Court for the Western District of Arkansas; and not a few others.

The staffs of many institutions have helped me in my search for material on the Hanging Judge. I would like to give special thanks to my friends at the Carnegie City Library and the United States District

---

[1] More properly, the United States Court for the Western District of Arkansas, having jurisdiction over the Indian Territory.

Court at Fort Smith; the National Archives and the Library of Congress in Washington, D.C.; the Wisconsin Historical Society, the Arkansas Historical Association, the Oklahoma Historical Society; the libraries of the University of Texas, the University of Arkansas, the University of Wisconsin.

The University of Arkansas and the University of Wisconsin have provided me with research grants.

The end-sheet map was drawn for this volume by James J. Flannery of the Geography Department of the University of Wisconsin.

This book is non-fiction. There are no imaginary conversations. The quotations are taken from contemporary sources.

Fred Harvey Harrington

Madison, Wisconsin
September 4, 1950

HANGING JUDGE

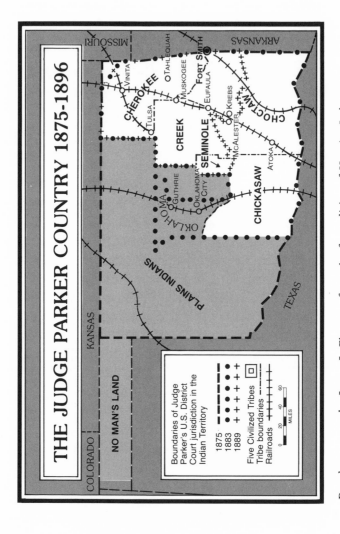

THE JUDGE PARKER COUNTRY 1875–1896

Boundaries of Judge
Parker's U.S. District
Court jurisdiction in the
Indian Territory

1875
1883
1889

☐ Five Civilized Tribes
---- Tribe boundaries
+++ Railroads

0 20 40 60
MILES

COLORADO

KANSAS

NO MAN'S LAND

MISSOURI

ARKANSAS

CHEROKEE

VINITA
TULSA
TAHLEQUAH
MUSKOGEE
FORT SMITH
EUFAULA
KREBS
McALESTER
ATOKA

CREEK

SEMINOLE

CHOCTAW

OKLAHOMA

GUTHRIE
OKLAHOMA CITY

CHICKASAW

PLAINS INDIANS

TEXAS

Based on a map by James J. Flannery from the first edition of *Hanging Judge*.

The barracks building (*left*), later used for Parker's court and jail, shown in an earlier view when Fort Smith was a fort in the Indian Territory. (Courtesy Fort Smith National Historic Site.)

Isaac C. Parker, as he appeared when appointed United States Judge in 1875. (Courtesy The Granger Collection, New York.)

Typical country cabin and road near Fort Gibson, characteristic of the Indian Territory during the Parker period. (Courtesy Archives and Manuscripts Division of the Oklahoma Historical Society.)

Deputy Marshal Heck Thomas, one of Parker's famous deputies *(seated at left)*, surrounded by another lawman, two Osage Indian scouts, and two court officers, ca. 1890. (Courtesy The Granger Collection, New York.)

Bill Powers, Bob Dalton, Grat Dalton and Dick Broadwell, after their attempted raid on two banks in Coffeyville, Kansas, October 1892. (Courtesy The Bettmann Archive.)

Belle Starr, as she appeared during her residence in the Indian country. (Courtesy Archives and Manuscripts Division of the Oklahoma
Historical Society.)

Belle Starr and her protégé, Blue Duck, photographed after Blue Duck's arrest for murder when Belle was in her late thirties. (Courtesy Archives and Manuscripts Division of the Oklahoma Historical Society.)

The old courthouse in Fort Smith, formerly the barracks building in the old fort, serving as a courtroom and a jail for the Parker court, 1872–88. (Courtesy Fort Smith National Historic Site.)

Prosecutor William H. H. Clayton, for fifteen years district attorney at Fort Smith, as he appeared when appointed Federal judge. (Courtesy Archives and Manuscripts Division of the Oklahoma Historical Society.)

Henry Starr, although twice convicted of murder, escaped the noose and was killed in an Arkansas bank holdup. (Courtesy The Bettmann Archive.)

Execution of Crawford Goldsby (Cherokee Bill) at Fort Smith, March 1895. (Courtesy Archives and Manuscripts Division of the Oklahoma Historical Society.)

A shackled Rufus Buck *(second from right)*, photographed with his gang while awaiting trial in 1895. (Courtesy The Granger Collection, New York.)

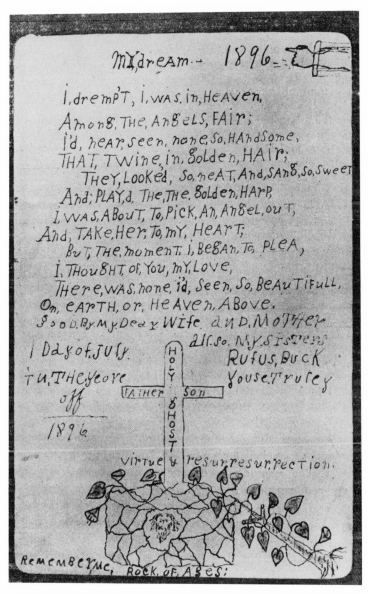

my dream -- 1896 --

i, drempt, i, was. in, Heaven,
Among, The, Angels, Fair;
i'd, hear, seen, none, so, Handsome,
That, Twine, in, Golden, Hair;
    They, Looked, so, neat, And, Sang, so, Sweet
And; PLAY,d, The, The, Golden, Harp,
i, was, About, To, Pick, An, Angel, out,
And, Take, Her, To, my, Heart;
    But, The, moment, i, Began, To, Plea,
i, Thought, of, You, my, Love,
There, was, none, i'd, Seen, so, Beautifull,
On, Earth, or, Heaven, Above.
Good, By, My, Dear, Wife, and, Mother
                        all, so, My, Sisters
i Day, of, July.   Rufus, Buck
                        HOLY
tu, Theyeore   Youse, Truley
off   Father   &   Son
                        GHOST
1896
        virtue & resur, resurrection.

Remember me, Rock, of, Ages;

Farewell note of Rufus Buck, written just before his execution and
discovered in his cell. (Courtesy Archives and Manuscripts Division
of the Oklahoma Historical Society.)

Saturday street scene in Muskogee, Indian Territory, at the close of the nineteenth century. (Courtesy Archives and Manuscripts Division of the Oklahoma Historical Society.)

Now in session, the new courtroom on Sixth Street in Fort Smith where Judge Parker held court from 1890–96. (Courtesy Fort Smith National Historic Site.)

Judge Isaac C. Parker, as he appeared at the end of his career. (Courtesy Fort Smith National Historic Site.)

CHAPTER ONE

Preying Wolves, Unfit to Live

Why . . . consign these men to death and exterminate them from the earth? Because they are preying wolves . . .unfit to live and unfit to remain at large.

—Western Independent, 1875

Children believe in Santa Claus; grownups believe in Robin Hood. They are sure that the great outlaws of the past robbed the rich to help the poor. They celebrate the names of the bad men of our Wild West—Billy the Kid, Jesse James, Bob Dalton, Cherokee Bill. These bandits, they maintain, were dashing, persecuted heroes who performed wondrous deeds with skill and courage.

This is not fact; it is fiction. The annals of our Wild West contain few wondrous deeds. The desperadoes of that frontier land were seldom brave or clever or kind or handsome. They were the persecutors, not the persecuted. They bled the rich, they bled the poor. They were ugly, selfish, sadistic brutes, as vile a lot of villains as ever took a stand against humanity.

Yes, it is time for us to change our heroes. We

should stop applying whitewash to such scoundrels as Bill Doolin, Belle Starr and the Verdigris Kid. Instead, we should honor the real heroes of the old frontier—men like Isaac Charles Parker, the United States judge who from 1875 to 1896 sent nearly eighty outlaws to the gallows.

> But was Judge Parker right to hang these men? Were they not victims of their environment, like the slum-bred delinquents of today? Did not these outlaws learn violence in the bloody Civil War?

Here we run into a magic name—William C. Quantrill. Like Heinrich Himmler, Quantrill taught school for a while. He won greater fame, however, as a Confederate irregular who had Cole Younger and the James boys in his band. The Civil War made this Quantrill a guerilla chieftain, and some of his men later became border bandits. The Civil War therefore contributed to border banditry.

But wait a minute. Quantrill was certainly a wicked man, one of the worst villains of his day. Yet it would be idle to suggest that he chose a career of crime because of the fight between the North and South. Quantrill was bad before the war began, and a bad man he remained. The confusion of the war years added to his opportunities; but he would have been a force for evil had there been no war at all.

No, it will not do to say that the frontier outlaws learned their tricks in the struggle between the Blue and Gray. For one thing, the Civil War was not a frontier conflict. Union and Confederate veterans did move out West in the years after the war. But, by and large, these former fighting men were peaceful citizens. Of the fourscore killers hanged by Judge Isaac Parker's order, only three had served in the Northern or Southern armies.

Now look at the other side. Judge Parker was a veteran. So was his most famous prosecutor, William Henry Harrison Clayton. Also his official hangman, George Maledon. And his court clerk. And most of the men who served as marshal in that district. And a good share of the deputy marshals, the "men who rode for Parker."

These men were veterans. The Civil War did not turn them into outlaws. It seems rather to have made them see the need for law and order.

Can the outlaws be defended on some other ground? What about the pastoral transition? Were cowboys thrown out of work and forced to turn to crime when the cattle range gave way to the farm?

This is an intriguing explanation; and it has some points. When Isaac Parker took up his judicial duties in the 1870's, the West still beckoned to the young. There was room in those days for a man to move around, for there was new land beyond the horizon. But less than a generation later people were saying that the frontier was gone, and that Americans had settled their broad acres from sea to sea.

Not only that: dirt farmers had pushed into the

19

cattle country, plowing up what had been the open range. In the process, some cowboys were squeezed out of work. They could, of course, have learned to till the soil; but some had no stomach for such humble work, and turned instead to crime.

Neat though this sounds, it does not give the whole answer. Despite the coming of the farmer, the cattle business held its own in many Western areas. It changed. The long drives ended as the railroads inched their way across the plains; and when barbed wire hit the market, ranchers fenced in their lands. But there was still work for the cow hand. And, even if the farmers did take over one region, there were ranches elsewhere. Moving was not hard for the average cowboy; hence there was nothing to compel him to turn bad.

Another point would seem to be in order. This discussion implies that most of the Western outlaws were ex-cowboys. So legend has it. In truth, many of the bad men were farmers or townspeople. Others were railroad workers, miners, lumbermen, professional bootleggers and tramps. There were cowboys, too, but few of them were unemployed, unless by choice.

How then can one explain the frontier bandit? Was he a man who breathed the individualistic spirit of a new land where all men cared for freedom and few for law?

This comes closer to it; but the statement gives the man of blood a better break than he deserves.

There was freedom on the frontier; but there was friendship, too. The Western people were self-confident, capable of making their own decisions. But at the same time they were friendly and co-operative. They liked and helped each other; they worked and played together. In doing so they built a good American tradition, one that combined personal liberty with community responsibility.

The desperado fitted only one side of this pattern. He was true to the frontier spirit of personal liberty; but he failed to understand the frontier spirit of community responsibility. He could be an individual, but he could not co-operate.

Put it in another way. It was easy to be bad in the old West. There were few law-enforcement officers, and one could carry weapons and no questions asked. And yet most border people behaved decently. The criminals were the ones too weak or stupid, too vicious, greedy, or unstable to withstand temptation.

Could that be? The storytellers picture the frontier outlaws as resourceful and brave.

Hanging Judge Parker, who knew these bandits by the thousand, spoke of them in other terms. He called them the "men of blood," the "wild men of the plain," the "refuse of humanity," "brutes . . . demons," with a "tigrish appetite for blood."

When asked to illustrate his point, His Honor named two men whom he considered typical frontier criminals. Both operated in Parker's jurisdiction—the

Indian country west of Arkansas, now the state of Oklahoma.

(1) Martin ("Bully") Joseph, with another horse thief, shot a partner from the rear, then raped and killed the dead man's wife. Joseph later disposed of his fellow murderer; but he could not keep his mouth shut. His boasts, and good detective work by Deputy Marshal J. H. Mershon led "Bully" to the gallows (1883).

(2) John Pointer rounded out a career of crime by butchering two friends and benefactors, splitting their skulls open with an ax. One of the victims, a crippled boy, was making breakfast for Pointer when the blow fell. Some said the murderer acted out of pure meanness (he was a nasty chap). More likely, Pointer killed to get his hands on his victims' property—a team of horses, a wagon, and a few supplies. After conviction before Judge Parker, John Pointer carried his case to the Supreme Court of the United States; but his appeal was rejected and he was hanged in 1894. His courage failed him in the death cell, and he proved a coward at the end.

> *But were these cases typical? Both these men were professional criminals who betrayed friends and killed in cold blood. Joseph's was a sordid sex crime; and Pointer took life for a very small return. Was Parker picking the most degraded specimens for his examples?*

No, the Judge was being fair. As Western outlaws went, Bully Joseph and John Pointer were about average.

Take the sex angle:

Sex offenses are rarely mentioned in the tales about the bad men of the Wild West; but such outrages loom large in the true story of frontier crime. Let us run through a few cases that turned up in Parker's court.

Matt Music, a married man, took liberties with a seven-year-old girl, giving the child a venereal disease. Music was tried, convicted, and sentenced to be hanged; but he managed to obtain a pardon from President Chester A. Arthur.

In another case, a white man was arrested for raping a seventy-year-old Cherokee squaw. The court reporters, who were far from squeamish, found the details presented at the trial so revolting as to be unprintable.

Old John Thornton repeatedly committed incest with his teen-aged daughter. "To get away from hell," the poor girl left home and married a young man of her acquaintance. Thornton showed up a week after the wedding, and, when the girl refused to resume their unnatural relations, shot her through the head. The hanging came in 1892, Thornton (who was sixty-five) being the oldest man hanged by Judge Parker's order.

One Andrew Latta seems to have seduced his sister and, when her child was born, to have helped her get rid of it. The baby was not killed outright but died of exposure. The penalty was three years in the penitentiary and a thousand-dollar fine.

Rufus Buck, a two-bit criminal who had served time for whisky peddling, decided to become a big-league bad man in 1895. Rounding up four other scoundrels, he formed the Buck gang, which operated chiefly in the Cherokee Nation. The gang was interested both in loot and in women. During a two-week period, its members held up several storekeepers and travellers, killed two persons (one of them a deputy) and raped at least two women. Convicted on a rape charge, all five were hanged together in 1896, perhaps the largest mass execution for rape in the history of the United States.

Did crime pay?

The notion persists that the frontier bandits often played for high stakes. In fact, the sums involved were often very small. Even with the famous outlaws the take was more frequently in two or three figures than in four or five.

One can check the fees of some of the men who killed for hire. In 1888, for instance, William Walker agreed to commit a murder in the Indian Territory for ten dollars and a half-gallon of whisky. He did the job and got the liquor but went to the gallows before he could collect the ten dollars.

Calvin James, a bootlegger, murdered a business associate in 1886 to get control of the stock on hand— four gallons of cheap whisky. He was hanged that same year.

In 1872 James Arcene and William Parchmeal committed murder for an even smaller sum. They waylaid and killed a traveller for his money, and found only twenty-five cents on the corpse. A deputy marshal

ran across the case a decade later, gathered evidence
and had both murderers executed in 1885.

Normally lawbreakers netted more than these four
characters. But the desperadoes rarely prospered.
Rustlers found it hard to unload stolen livestock at
good prices. Fear of capture kept holdup men from
operating regularly, and their cash did not last long
when they were on the scout. All but a handful were
short of funds when they were taken into custody.
So it was with minor outlaws, also with such well-
known figures as Bill Cook and Belle Starr.

*Lust and greed were not all the story; hate
was a factor, too.*

Frontier folklore makes much of this. The outlaw
burned with a desire to get revenge, an urge to right
wrongs done to him or his loved ones. As the story
grows, the wrong becomes "an insult worse than
death," and the desperado seems almost justified in
doing in his enemy.

In reality, the "wrong" was generally an imagined
insult or a petty slight that should have been forgotten. Look at three of the cases that came before
Judge Parker.

Bill Brown beat Bob Moore in a frontier foot race,
winning a fifty-cent side bet. An argument ensued,
and Moore thrashed Brown badly. Humiliated, Brown
rushed out, grabbed a gun and lay waiting for his foe.
But in the excitement Brown fired at the first man
who came along—not Moore, but Brown's own friend,
Ralph Tate. In court Brown sought acquittal on the

ground that the killing of Tate was an error. Isaac Parker brushed this plea aside, and Brown was hanged in a five-man execution in 1881.

When drunk, one day, Kit Ross rode his horse into the cabin of Jonathan Davis. Davis expelled the intruder, who nursed a grudge thereafter.

Two years later, the pair met in a country store.

"Kit, I believe we are going to have some snow," said Davis.

"Yes," said Ross, "I think we are," and pumped two shots into Davis' back.

Ross was hanged in 1886.

With Eli Lucas the motive was even feebler. An idiot boy was annoying other spectators at a baseball game. Finally he went away. Lucas followed, shot the lad and returned to the ball game. After the last inning he again sought his victim. The boy was not yet dead and begged for a drink of water. Instead of getting it, Lucas fired again and as the half-wit struggled to get away, the murderer dispatched him with a final shot.

Anxious to be called a "killer," Lucas boasted of his deed. He was arrested, convicted and sentenced to be hanged (1895). The Supreme Court, however, set aside the verdict on jurisdictional grounds; and Eli Lucas went free.

Turn next to hospitality and loyalty:

It is often said that the bad men of the West, for all

their faults, were loyal to their friends and grateful to anyone who gave them food and shelter.

Let us see.

One evening just before Christmas, 1880, two strangers stopped at Eli McVay's one-room log cabin. Although his family had retired McVay gladly took the travellers in, for it was cold and "Mac" was a friendly man. The visitors, he said, could spend the night by the fire.

At two or three in the morning McVay crawled out of bed to take care of his twin babies, who were ill. His guests got up at the same time. One of them asked for tobacco; then the other, without any provocation whatever, opened fire on his host.

"Oh, Lord!" cried McVay as he slumped, dying, to the floor.

The visitors then turned to Bill Barnett, McVay's hired hand. The first bullet missed its mark; the second grazed the side of Barnett's head. Though stunned, Barnett found his way to his feet and grabbed one of his assailants. But the other seized an ax, and with a series of brutal blows severed Barnett's right hand and cut deep gashes in the poor man's neck and back and legs.

Thinking Barnett dead, the murderers went after Mrs. McVay, who was holding her two babies. But then a dog barked loudly, and the cutthroats went out to see if any one was coming. Mrs. McVay seized the chance to slip away. Clad only in her nightdress, and clutching her twins in her arms, she ran nearly a mile across the frozen ground to the house of a neighbor.

"They have killed poor Mac," she screamed as she

approached the house, "and split Barnett's head open."

Strange to say, Barnett was still living. He regained consciousness after Mrs. McVay had fled. He knew that he was bleeding badly but did not realize that his right hand was missing until he reached for a gun. And yet he managed to escape. Later he and Mrs. McVay identified the killers—Amos and Abner Manly —and the pair was hanged in 1881.

Exceptional? Hardly; frontier bad men made a specialty of turning on their hosts and travelling companions. That was the easy way. The victims, thinking they were with friends, could be caught unawares.

Nor did the lawbreakers stick together, despite all tales of gang discipline and honor among thieves. Take the case of John Wodiver, alias John Robinson. A liquor smuggler, horse thief, and killer, Wodiver had many friends among the criminals of the Southwest frontier. But then, in 1884, he was badly wounded in a drunken brawl. It was widely known that he was hurt and needed help; but in this crisis the injured man was totally abandoned by his outlaw friends. A few ordinary citizens supplied food and water. The bad men stayed away.

Left alone in a dirty outhouse, Wodiver slept in his own filth for a month and a half, his wounds uncleaned and undressed. Being paralyzed below the waist, he could not even cope with the rats, which gnawed off two of his toes.

Wodiver was rescued, not by another man of crime, but by Deputy Marshal Mershon of the Parker court. Taking pity on the invalid, Captain Mershon hired a wagon and hauled Wodiver two hundred miles to the jail hospital in Fort Smith, Arkansas. There the man died, still unnoticed by his friends.

This story of indifference can be matched by many of betrayal. Time after time Western bandits turned against each other to save their own necks. This was a great help to Judge Parker, for, when former partners denounced each other in court, the law often won a double victory. ("In order that there might be no mistake, the jury found them both guilty," ran a typical press comment, "They are both bad eggs.")

> *They were "bad eggs," "very hard cases," men of "great depravity and great wickedness." They acted out of burning lust, unholy greed or "pure unadulterated meanness." They were "preying wolves unfit to live."*

So wrote the crime reporters who attended sessions of Judge Parker's court. These reporters were not deceived by legends. They based their stories on what they saw. And, seeing frontier bad men every day, they knew, and said, that Robin Hood did not ride the Western plains.

CHAPTER TWO

Listen Now to the Dreadful Sentence

*I sentence you ... to be hanged by the neck until
dead. And may God, whose laws you have broken ...
have mercy on your soul.*

—Judge Isaac Parker

The crowd came early lest it miss the show. Men had
stretched rope before in this dreary little border city
of Fort Smith. But this time, on September 3, 1875,
six were to die at once, all hanging in a row. And it
was whispered that these six were only the beginning
of the gallows fruit of Isaac Parker, a new and terrify-
ing judge who was set on bringing law and order to
the Southwest frontier.

In passing sentence Judge Parker had ordered execution, not at dawn or dusk, but in the full light of day.
Some time from nine to five, His Honor had decreed.
Jim Fagan, as United States Marshal, could name the
exact hour and choose a "convenient place."

Jim of course had decided to use the gallows down
by the southwest wall of what had been the Federal
military garrison. This gallows was well located,

30

being a hundred and fifty yards from the dilapidated barracks building which housed the Parker court and jail. And there would be no squeeze for space. The platform had been built for size (fourteen by fifteen feet); and the great crossbeam of seasoned oak could handle a dozen condemned men at a time. Besides, the gallows was out in the open, providing a good view for the spectators who began gathering in the early morning.

It was to be a well-reported hanging. The local reporters were present, and others from Little Rock, St. Louis and faraway New York. Strange crowd, thought the big-city correspondents. There were white people, Negroes, and Indians, and every mixture of these three. There were farmers in working clothes, and well-dressed city folk, and rough-clad frontiersmen.

Some of those present were from Fort Smith and other parts of Arkansas. Rather more were from the turbulent Indian country to the west. For the Parker court, though domiciled in Arkansas, was important chiefly because it had jurisdiction, westward, over seventy thousand square miles of frontier territory. From that troubled land came most of the prisoners who appeared in Parker's United States Court for the Western District of Arkansas, including the six men who were to hang that day.

The crowd was noisy at the start, but settled down as the guards appeared. Yes, that was Hangman Maledon, that slouchy-looking little man. Didn't look like much, but he was careful. You could see that as he gave the six ropes a final check.

Smart to do that. A Mississippi hangman had botched his job the month before.

"Don't choke me!" the bleeding victim had screamed as the scaffold collapsed, "Jesus save me!"

They had hanged him all right, on the second try. But George Maledon wanted none of that on his record. Nor did Judge Parker: messy work created sympathy for murderers.

Hear those noises from the jail? That was the clank of hammer against chisel as the foot shackles were removed. Then silence, while the condemned men ate their final meal and put on their hanging clothes.

There were six of them—Smoker Mankiller and Sam Fooy, Heck Campbell and John Whittington, Dan Evans and James Moore. Two others had been earmarked for the gallows by the Hanging Judge. One, a teen-aged boy, had had his sentence changed to life imprisonment by Ulysses S. Grant, the President of the United States. The other had "gone before," cut down by rifle fire while trying to escape. (The rifle, by the way, had been fired by George Maledon, who was as handy with a gun as with a noose.)

For the six remaining there would be neither flight nor commutation. Marshal Fagan lined them up at half-past nine, then marched them—double file—out of his grimy jail and towards the waiting gallows. Four local clergymen led the sad procession, and well-armed guards fell in at the sides and rear.

"DIE BRAVE!" So reads the code of doomed men, good and bad, in every corner of the earth. It will not do to show emotion, to falter in the shadow of the scaffold, to quail before the crowd.

Parker's frontier sextette ran true to form.

"Come life, or death, 'tis all the same to me," they seemed to say as they trudged their last hundred yards, climbed their last dozen steps and looked up at the dangling ropes.

There was Sam Fooy, whispered a spectator; he was the smart one. A quarter-Cherokee, the papers said, though he looked all white, with his pale face and his hazel eyes and auburn hair. They said he had religion. That was natural in a man about to die, but Sam had caught faith with a vengeance. He had bent his knees in prayer many times as the end came near, had learned a lot of hymns and had talked about such things as sin and salvation.

I dreamed that I was on the gallows before a great crowd of people [Sam had told a reporter a day or two before the execution] I was sick and weak, and felt like fainting, and I thought I could not face death. Just then a fellow stepped up from the crowd, came right to me and said: 'Look here, Sam, don't you be afraid to let them jump you. Jesus is standing under the floor, and he will catch you in his arms.'

I felt strong and when the drop came I felt no pain, but fell asleep, and woke up in a beautiful garden—the most beautiful place I ever saw, with running waters and stars dancing on the waves.

Yes, that was Sam Fooy, quite a talker . . . but he was silent as he sat on the rough bench at the rear of the platform and listened to the reading of the six death warrants.

Had he last words to say?

"I am as anxious to get out of this world," was his reply, "as the people who have come here today are to see me. I will not delay you."

Most of the others chose to speak a little longer when they had their turns—James Moore, for instance, a white man who, in height and reputation, towered over all his gallows partners. Moore looked gigantic on the platform, a tall broad-shouldered man with bulging muscles. He seemed immobile now, his thin lips tightly closed, his gray eyes in repose. But it was said that he could move with speed, as fast as any desperado in the border country. In proving that, James Moore had become a famous, almost a legendary figure along the Southwest frontier.

The crowd pressed forward eagerly to catch his final words. Moore's had been a life of excitement, daring and adventure. Would he display bravado to the end?

He would. Gazing down upon his last audience, James Moore spoke his piece in clear, crisp tones:

"I have lived like a man, and I will die like a man. I am prepared . . . I think I see men here who are worse than I have ever been. I hope you may make peace with God before brought to my condition."

Like Moore, John (or William) Whittington was a white man. There resemblance ended. James Moore was tall and fair, the very picture of good health. John Whittington was dark, darker than the quarter-breed Sam Fooy. He was of average height; was lean and sallow-faced, and his bright eyes shone with the sickness that had bothered him in jail.

Ill, and concerned about his family, John Whittington had decided that he would not be up to speaking when he stood under the noose. He had therefore

told his story to his spiritual adviser; and this clergy-
man, the Reverend H. M. Granade, read the words
when Whittington's turn came:

How I Came to the Gallows

My father taught me to be honest and avoid all those great
sins that disgrace the world. But he did not teach me to be
religious ... He showed me how to drink whisky ... and that is
what brought me to the gallows ... If I had been blessed with the
good instruction that I have had since I have been in prison I
would have been a good and happy man today with my family. O!
What will become of my poor wife and two little boys, who are
away out on Red River!

I fear that people will slight them, and compel them to go into
low bad company, on account of the disgrace that I have brought
upon them. But I leave them in the hands of that gracious God
in whom I have learned to trust, and who has freely and fully
pardoned all my sins for Jesus' sake. Into his hands I now com-
mend my soul, fully believing that I shall this day be in heaven.

O! that men would leave off drinking altogether! And O
Parents! I send forth this dying warning to you today, standing
on this gallows. Train up your children in the way they should go,
my father's example brought me to ruin. God love us all. Farewell! farewell.

These three—Fooy, Moore and Whittington—had
not denied their guilt. The other three used their last
words to insist upon their innocence. It was as though
they still hoped for reprieve or looked upon the motley
throng of spectators as a special jury or a sort of court
of last appeal.

Dan Evans was a young white man, well-built, and
handsome in a jaunty way, with his curly hair and his
soft blue eyes. He was a flippant one, murmured a
reporter; he had sassed the Hanging Judge for fair.
For back in June, when sentenced to be hanged, Dan
had bowed to Isaac Parker and had cried out "Thank

ye" in a mocking way. Then he had turned his back upon the bench of judgment, to laugh and joke with other prisoners. On the gallows platform he had the same dash and defiance, the same self-confident determination.

Heck Campbell was a Negro, short and stocky, younger even than was Evans. The crowd viewed Heck with interest, knowing that it was his half-brother who had died while trying to break jail. Knowing too that Heck's last visitor had been his mother, who had brought him cookies and a candy stick and some home-grown tobacco.

Heck was calm and cool as he neared the end.

"I did not shoot anybody," he said simply, "I am innocent and ready to die."

Smoker Mankiller was an Indian, a glum and pock-marked Cherokee with thick, full lips and dull black eyes. Since he could, or would, not use the white man's language, his death warrant was read both in English and in Cherokee. The Indian then addressed the crowd in his own tongue An interpreter translated, lest any one be left in doubt as to Mankiller's sentiments.

"I am prepared to die . . ." the comment ran, "I did not kill Short; I would acknowledge it if I had. I have never been guilty of a mean act in my life. I killed a Cherokee; but I killed him in self-defence . . . My conviction was caused by prejudice and false testimony."

With the warrants read and the talking over, the preliminaries were nearly at an end. Reverend Sample spoke a brief, impressive prayer. The doomed men joined their voices in two hymns which seemed to fit the occasion—*Come Let Us Join Our Friends Above* and *Nearer My God To Thee*. Then, after hands were clasped for one last time, black robes were wrapped around the prisoners. Arms were bound securely with stout cord and the condemned men were moved to their assigned positions. Guards adjusted the black caps that were to shut out the light forever, and slipped on the nooses.

"Lord Jesus receive me," called one of those about to die. Sam Fooy, more than likely, but there was no telling, for just then the trap was sprung.

No one struggled. Every neck was broken.

It was a gruesome sight: six limp and lifeless bodies dangling from their gallows cords. It was not easy to forget the faces of the doomed—Heck Campbell protesting his innocence, Sam Fooy dreaming of eternity, John Whittington worrying about his family.

Queer business, mumbled some of the spectators as they shuffled off to Fort Smith's saloons. Were they so bad, these men whom Parker hanged? Or was the Judge the bad one, coming from Washington to interfere with the free life of the frontier?

At least one observer had the answer. This was W. J. Weaver of the *Western Independent*. Weaver knew the frontier outlaws well; he was later to be known as the confidant of Belle Starr and the Dalton brothers.

Naturally said Weaver, "morbid curiosity ... absorbs the mind in witnessing an event so rare and tragical." But "the moral should not be lost in the excitement and glare of the terrible exhibition." These six men had been hanged for "preying ... upon the lives and property of their fellow beings." And Judge Isaac Parker, in ordering their execution, was trying to protect the decent people, so that the Southwest might become a great and decent land.

This Judge Parker had few tears for those who died upon the scaffold. His tears were for the innocent, for the victims, for the families of the murdered men.

When their son came, Isaac Parker's parents gave him a name from the Old Testament. And, as a frontier judge, Parker looked to the Holy Book for inspiration.

"The Court is but the humble instrument," he said, "to aid in the execution of that divine justice which has ever decided that he who takes what he cannot return —human life—shall lose his own."

Would it have been better if His Honor had paid more attention to the Biblical passages about forgiveness?

For an answer, look at the record of the star actors in the sextuple hanging of 1875.

The first one sentenced was John Whittington, he who was to impress the gallows crowd with his touching devotion to his wife and children. Whittington's was a crime of passion and of greed, committed out in the Choctaw Nation one Sunday afternoon. He and an aged neighbor named John Turner had gone across the border to a Texas rumshop and were returning home well filled with bargain whisky. Turner, as his companion knew, had a hundred and five dollars on his person. So, picking up a heavy club, Whittington struck his friend from the rear, knocking the old man to the ground and clubbing him into insensibility.

Then, pulling out his bowie knife, the assailant slashed Turner's throat from ear to ear.

The man you murdered, was your friend [said Judge Parker in pronouncing judgment] and you had spent most of the Sabbath day . . . in his company. In an unsuspecting hour when he no doubt was treating you as a trusted friend you stole upon him unperceived and aimed the deadly weapon at his head and with the fateful knife you brutally hacked his throat to pieces and with these fatal instruments of death, you mangled, you murdered your victim.

But your guilt and your depravity did not stop there. Scarcely had you committed the bloody deed before you entered upon the commission of another crime. You converted to your person as spoils of the murder your victim's money.

Like many another criminal, Whittington had hoped to get away. But Turner's son had seen the killing from a distance. Racing up, he found the still-bleeding body of his father. Whittington had hurried off, taking his victim's cash and rifle; but in his haste the slayer had left his blood-stained knife behind. And there was blood on his hat and on his hands when he was taken prisoner.

To most border people, the arrest was credited to young Turner, who had taken up the chase before the trail was cold. But to Judge Isaac Parker the capture had a broader meaning. His Honor said as much when he read the death sentence. Looking down upon the prisoner, Parker spoke with severity:

As God himself has prescribed the righteous penalty for this offense, so there is strong reason to believe that very few murders are committed which are not ultimately discovered and the wicked perpetrators finally, if not by law by some other agency, brought to merited punishment. . . .

Debased and unfortunate man! ... You forgot that the eye of your God was fixed upon you; the eye of that God who suffers not even a sparrow to fall without His notice.

You forgot that you were in the presence of Heaven to whom the light of day and darkness of night are the same.

Though an irresponsible drunkard, Whittington was no professional desperado. But that term fitted several of his gallows partners. Dan Evans, for one. A brutal, reckless youth, Evans had early turned to evil. As a boy still in his teens, he had helped Jim Reed (Belle Starr's first "husband") rob Watt Grayson in the Creek Nation. It was known that Old Watt had several thousand dollars in gold coin. When he would not tell where the money was hidden, Reed and Evans forced him to talk under torture, jabbing lighted pine sticks into the old man's flesh.

Dan was not hanged for that, but for a killing of 1874, near Eufaula, in the country of the Cherokees. He was seen riding with a one-eyed man, Bill Seabolt. Then Evans was seen alone, leading his friend's gray horse and wearing Seabolt's hat, boots, and spurs. A little later the local people found a bullet-riddled corpse. The body was too badly decomposed to be identified with ease, but there was a patch over the left eye, and near by was a memo book in which Seabolt had signed his name.

Arrested, Evans hired a crack lawyer, putting up Seabolt's horse as part of the counsel fee. Mistaken identity, the defense maintained, an error all round. But then the victim's father came in from Texas; and, in the language of Evans' lawyer, "the . . . defendant was surprised by the introduction of material testimony against him, which he was wholly unable to anticipate, and consequently to rebut."

To be specific, the senior Seabolt carefully described the horseshoe nails in his son's boots. The startled Evans, as every juror saw, was wearing boots that fitted this exact description.

James Moore was also a professional, and a bully and a braggart, too. He was defiant when he was wounded and taken prisoner. Sure he was an outlaw, and he was proud of it. He had shot eight white men in his day, plus many Indians and "niggers"—he never kept a count of those.[1] Yes, he was of good family, but he liked the wild life and would return to banditry when he got out of jail.

Well, said Judge Parker, James Moore would not get out this time. Instead he would measure space beneath the crossbeam of the Fort Smith gallows.

Parker then ran through Moore's record. He had been lucky, had long managed to evade the law. His luck turned when he and his partner Hunton stole some horses from a lame farmer in northwest Arkansas. A posse pursued the horse thieves across the border into the Indian country. There Moore and Hunton brought down two of their pursuers, slaying Deputy Marshal William Spivey near the Little Blue River, and wounding popular Captain A. D. Irwin. The bandits then managed to get away.

Captured soon after, Hunton turned state's evi-

---

[1] This was a standard boast of frontier bad men and should not be taken literally. There was much race prejudice in the Southwest; but the desperadoes counted all their victims and added a few for good measure.

dence in the hope of getting better treatment than he deserved. Confession did not help him much, for he was filled with lead in an attempt to escape from his captors. But Hunton's testimony enabled Federal officers to track down James Moore. Moore was arrested while he was getting ready to kill a cattle drover who was taking cattle through the Indian Territory to market in Missouri.

It was a pity, said Parker, to waste talents such as Moore's. Still, the Judge went on, "sympathy should not be reserved wholly for the criminal. I believe in standing on the side of the innocent . . . quiet, peaceable, law-abiding citizen. Is there no sympathy for him?" Could one turn loose the unregenerate and incorrigible, the men like this James Moore, who boasted of his sins?

Smoker Mankiller was aptly named—he had killed two men before he came of age. His murder of another Cherokee took him into tribal court, for Parker had no jurisdiction in cases involving only Indians. This meant acquittal. The red man's tribunals, like the ecclesiastical courts of old, were noted for their leniency. ("There never is any one convicted in the nation for such a trifle as killing anybody.")

Had that been all Mankiller might have lived a while. But he also killed a white man, his neighbor, William Short. While the motive was obscure, it was apparant that the Indian had asked to see Short's gun and then had fired the weapon at point-blank range. In all probability, Short had died at once; but, just to make sure, Smoker Mankiller had drawn his knife and hacked his neighbor into ribbons.

Parker sometimes wound up a murder trial in a morning and an afternoon. Because of the language problem, the Mankiller case took a bit longer—nearly three whole days. But it ended like the others.

"The law has come on me," said the gloomy Cherokee.

"Indeed," snapped Isaac Parker, "the sword of human justice trembles over you and is about to fall upon your guilty head."

There were three defendants in Heck Campbell's case—Heck (who was really Edmund), his brother Sam, and their half-brother, Frank Butler. This was a feuding matter, the Butler-Campbell clan having had troubles with one Lawson Ross, out in the Choctaw country. Conflict had moved into the ugly stage after a prayer-meeting brawl; then Lawson Ross had been murdered in his bed. While doing that, the brothers had also butchered Maria McKinney, a girl who lived with Ross. It was a cowards' killing; the victims had no chance at all.

Sam Campbell, who was very young, came out with a six-year prison term for manslaughter. The other two were convicted of murder; but, Frank Butler having been killed in his jail break, only Heck Campbell was sentenced.

Heck would not say much when he was called before Judge Parker to hear his fate. Talk would not mean anything, he grunted, though he still hoped that

President Grant would save him from death on the gallows.

Wait a minute, said Judge Parker. Why should the White House give its blessing to the mean and the malicious? Heck Campbell had better not delude himself with thoughts of escape or clemency. Let him rather think about his crime and get ready to meet his Maker.

> In my judgment your destiny in this world is fixed, [said the Judge] and your fate is inevitable. . . .
> Let me therefore beg of you to fly to Him for that mercy and that pardon which you cannot expect of mortals.
> When you return to the solitude of your prison . . . bring to your recollection the mortal struggles and dying groans of your murdered victim. . . .
> And when by such reflections as these your heart shall become softened . . . fly for mercy to the arms of the Savior and endeavor to seize upon the salvation of His Cross.
> Listen now to the dreadful sentence of the law and then farewell forever until the court and you and all here today shall meet together in the general resurrection.

Sam Fooy, Parker felt, was even less deserving of a pardon. He could have gone the way of his sister's husband, Captain C. R. Stevenson, a deputy marshal of the Fort Smith court. Fooy, however, chose to be a gambler, thief, and drunkard, closing his career of crime with the murder of an unarmed schoolteacher.

"Pale death treads with even steps the hovels of the poor and the palaces of kings."

These words, from the first book of Horace, were written in the notebook found beside the skeleton out by the Illinois River. The book also gave the dead man's name, John Emmett Naff.

"No other young man that was ever reared in our town possessed natural gifts superior to his," testified the *Jonesboro Journal,* from Naff's home in Tennessee. "He lacked steadiness and application to make his life a succession of brilliant successes." But, being of "erratic disposition," John Emmett had preferred a "wandering and adventurous life," which in time took him to the Indian Territory. There he was known as the "barefoot school teacher," a drifter, but a likeable and useful person.

Naff wound up a school term near Tahlequah in the summer of 1872 and was paid two hundred and fifty dollars by the school board. Then he packed his clothes and books and walked away. His last stop was at the home of Sam Fooy's brother-in-law, Deputy Marshal Stevenson. Fooy, who was visiting his sister, noted that the teacher pulled out a five-dollar bill when it was time to pay his fifty cents for bed and board. Sam then decided to leave with the departing guest. On the trip he bashed in Naff's skull and made off with his victim's clothes and money.

Sam's loose tongue brought him to his doom. No one saw him do his bloody deed and the corpse was not found for a full year. But Fooy told his sordid tale to relatives and babbled in the brothels and saloons along the border.

Sam Fooy made a grand impression in the Fort Smith jail. Cheerful and friendly, he was liked both by the inmates and by the visitors. The guards called him a model prisoner; the Fort Smith preachers spoke of his co-operative spirit; the local ladies showered him with bouquets, fruit, and sympathy.

Too bad, said Judge Parker.

"The good ladies who carry flowers and jellies to criminals mean well . . ." His Honor added. "But what mistaken goodness! They see the convict . . . They forget the crime he perpetrated . . . by his assassin work."

Look at Fooy; look at Naff. It was a rough new country to the west, a land that needed learning, law, and decency. Who could supply those needs? Was it the gay and carefree Fooy, he of the liquor shops and gambling dens and bawdyhouses, he who admitted that he had broken all the Ten Commandments? Or was it Naff, the simple travelling teacher, he who brought books to the Southwest frontier, and helped the younger generation prepare for a brighter future?

There, right there was the key to Fort Smith's scaffold justice. Men could cry cruelty and shudder at the gallows business. But as Judge Isaac Parker frowned down upon his prisoners he thought of the John Emmett Naffs and of the fate of generations yet to come.

Sentimentalists might find romance in the wild and blood-stained ruffians who set law at defiance on the old frontier. Judge Parker found only wasted opportunities, misspent lives, drabness, degradation, villainy, threats to all that he held dear. Thus he spoke with firmness to this killer, Fooy, and to many dozen others who stood before his bar of justice.

Crime is crime, and the murderer must be punished as an example to others. Screening him from punishment is the greatest calamity to the members of society, and the murderer must look to a Higher Court, to a Higher Power, to a Higher Law, for mercy, for absolute forgiveness.

LISTEN NOW TO THE DREADFUL SENTENCE

You have taken human life. You have sent a soul unprepared to its Maker. You have set at defiance God's law.

The sentence of the law is that you be taken to the jail from whence you came, there to be closely and securely kept until the day of execution . . . then to be hanged by the neck until dead.

And may God, whose laws you have broken and before whose dread tribunal you must then come have mercy on your soul.

CHAPTER THREE

Let No Guilty Man Escape

In the administration of the law for the Indian Terri-
tory, Judge Parker was a necessity. The Almighty
created him for a purpose.

—Prosecutor W. H. H. Clayton

In truth, it was accident that took Isaac Charles Parker to the Southwest frontier. But for chance, he might have gone to Utah to hand down law among the Mormons.

Parker's early life was not sensational. He was born in rural Ohio on October 15, 1838. While helping on the farm he got in a few winters of grade school and some work at an academy that was perhaps as advanced as a junior high school of today. Isaac then taught country school; and, after racing through a few law books, won admission to the Ohio bar. That was in 1859, the year he came of age.

Then the young man caught the Western fever. Not that Ohio was overcrowded; but moving West was a tradition in those days. Isaac's father had drifted in from Pennsylvania, and his father's people had gone

48

there from Massachusetts. Isaac's mother's folks had
come West from Virginia. Hence it was natural for
the young lawyer to push along. He hung out his
shingle in St. Joseph, Missouri.

Some went further west, to Kansas and beyond.
But Parker liked St. Joe. There he met and fell in love
with pretty Mary O'Toole. Parker was a Protestant,
Mary a Roman Catholic—which fact delayed, but did
not prevent, a marriage that proved most successful.
Parker worshipped his dark-eyed cheerful Mary, was
devoted to her and their two sons. And Mary found
her Isaac perfect, a kind and loving husband, an in-
dulgent father.

While courting Mary, Parker plunged into politics.
He had the background for it. He was related to
William Shannon, who had been governor of Ohio
and Kansas. Like Uncle Bill, Parker began as a Demo-
crat, wedded to the tradition of Thomas Jefferson
and Andrew Jackson. His living hero was the Little
Giant, Stephen A. Douglas of Illinois. Parker set up
Douglas Clubs in Missouri and in the 1860 presidential
race did his best to help Douglas beat that other
Illinoisan, Abraham Lincoln.

When Lincoln won and the South seceded, there
was a crisis in the border states. Should Missouri, like
other slave states, join the Confederacy? Or should
it stay with the Union? As a Northerner, a nonslave-
holder, and a Douglas man, Parker chose the Union.
He saw military service, of the home-guard type, and
used his politician's skill to keep Missouri on the
Northern side.

As his reputation grew, the St. Joe lawyer was

chosen city attorney, then circuit court attorney. During the Reconstruction era, when just thirty years of age, he was elected judge of the Twelfth Judicial District of Missouri. In 1870 he quit the bench to run for Congress. He won; and two years later he was re-elected.

Meantime Parker had changed his party label. A Democrat when the Civil War began, he gave full support to Abraham Lincoln's Republican administration. When the President sought re-election, in 1864, Parker was a Lincoln presidential elector. Presently he left the Democrats for good, and as a Congressman he was a regular Republican.

By that time Parker rated party favors, such as a nomination for the United States Senate (1874). This was in the nature of a compliment, for Missouri had gone Democratic and no Republican could hope to win. Nor could Parker try for re-election to the House that fall; despite his personal popularity, he could not have hoped to win. It was understood, however, that he would get an appointment from the White House when he retired from Congress in March, 1875. Sure enough, President Grant appointed him Chief Justice of Utah Territory.

Parker then took the most important step of his career. He wrote the President asking that he be named, instead, judge of the United States Court for the Western District of Arkansas. While the Utah job had a more high-sounding title, it had many drawbacks. For one thing, Utah was far away. For another, the post was temporary—Territorial officers would cease to function when Utah became a state. The

Arkansas post, on the other hand, was for life ("good behavior") and Fort Smith was not so terribly far from Parker's beloved St. Joe.

In writing the White House, Parker said that he could do the job. He knew the law; Grant could check on that. He had served on the bench, as judge of an important Missouri circuit. And he would fit the needs of Fort Smith better than an Eastern man. He lived in a region not unlike western Arkansas; and, having specialized in Indian affairs in Congress, he knew the problems of a court that had been given jurisdiction over the vast Indian country west of Arkansas.

He got the job. Though none too bright in picking his subordinates, Ulysses S. Grant did see Parker's talents. Then, too, the President knew that the Republicans were in a sorry fix in the Southwest. After a brief period of victories, they had begun to slip. Their decline had been hastened by rumors, and evidence, of corruption in state and local offices. Scandal had hit the Fort Smith court, and Judge William Story had quit under fire. To make up for that, and to redeem the reputation of the party, Grant had to appoint a forceful and incorruptible outsider. Isaac Parker seemed to fill the bill. He was very young to be a district judge, only thirty-six; but he was honest and a fighter.

The President did not expect that Parker would want the job for very long.

"Stay a year or two," Grant said, "and get things straightened out."

"I did not expect to stay here more than a year or

two . . ." Parker told a reporter two decades later, "but I am still here, as you see."

"Yes, it was the greatest mistake of your life," said the Judge's wife, adding, to the interviewer, "He is only fifty-eight but he looks like a very old man."

"No, Mary, not a mistake," said Parker, "for we have been enabled to arrest the flood tide of crime."

Judge and Mrs. Parker and their children reached Fort Smith on a pleasant Sunday morning, May 2, 1875. The family had come by steamboat, up the shallow, winding Arkansas, for there was as yet no railroad to the border city.

Being realists, the newcomers expected little in the way of progress or comforts. They found less than that. In 1875 Fort Smith was a sorry little settlement of less than three thousand souls. Even boosters admitted that it was "a town of the second class," and it was hard to find a booster. There were no paved streets, no sidewalks, no street lights save for a lantern here and there. There were no factories, no good hotels, no decent public schools. Garrison Avenue was broad enough, Lord knows, but rain made it "nasty and uninviting," a "seething mass of mud and filth," "simply a mud hole with all the garnishments needed to complete its filthy grotesqueness." When the sun shone, as it did on the day of Parker's arrival, there was dust to baffle the pedestrian or to drive him into the saloons, of which Fort Smith had more than enough.

Oh well, agreed the Parkers, this frontier town was for the future rather than the past. Surely there were friendly people here; many had gathered at the docks to welcome the newcomers. The Judge and Mary had been pleased at that and had given pleasure in return. ("We were charmed," was the verdict on both sides, "and delighted every way.")

Time would confirm the first impression. The Parkers found that most Fort Smith people made first-rate neighbors and were interested in schools, hospitals, and peaceful progress. Parker's problem area was the wild country to the west, but many of his deputies and jurors came from Fort Smith. Without help from these Arkansawyers, the Judge would have been hamstrung. With their aid he was able to attack the problem of crime on the frontier and to work toward his ideal, "a great government where liberty, regulated by law, would be guaranteed to all, even the humblest."

When Isaac Parker reached Fort Smith he found his court "permeated with official corruption," "disorganized, uncapable, corrupt—a source of laughter for the law-breaking, a by-word among the people, and a reproach to American institutions." Those out in the Indian country suffered most, with lawlessness unchecked and crime unpunished. But Fort Smith felt it, too, with court officials taking bribes within the city, with open stealing from the marshal's funds, with bandits riding in from the West to bellow in the barrooms and strut in the shadow of the Federal gallows.

Then came Parker. The decent people and the grafters both looked him over. A tall, big-shouldered man with piercing eyes, a quick, firm step, a bold, determined jaw. The guess was that this judge was not a weakling or corruptionist but a man who would have his own way.

The proof came quickly, when Parker opened court eight days after he reached town.

"A vast improvement over . . . the notorious Story," said a local paper, the *New Era*, during Parker's first term of court, "and as yet we have never heard a word of complaint against him from any quarter, either as regards his competency, impartiality or courtesy."

Later, as convictions mounted, the tributes were much stronger.

"The history of the United States court for the Indian country is his history, its annals are his biography," said one, and "the wonder of its story is an admiration for his achievements."

"His place will be among the few great men of the century," said another, and still another rated Parker as "one of the truly great and strong men of the age."

All that, in token of his work on the bench. But it was when he doffed his robe that friends liked Parker best. Then he could set aside the stern and unforgiving manner of the Hanging Judge, and be plain Isaac Parker, a sweet-tempered, charming man.

"Although he was a terror to the criminals," said one who knew him well, "he had a heart as tender as a child's."

"His friendships were eternal," said colleagues, he was the "best and truest of men," a "truly noble character," "one of the finest men who ever lived."

Outsiders often wondered how there could be gentleness in one who kept the hangman busy.

Why not, replied the Judge's friends? It was love

for right and good that made Parker fight the "red handed demon," murder. Or put it another way. Parker disapproved of "mob law." By this he meant ordinary mob action (lynching, Southern fashion) and also vigilante work (lynching, Western style). Arrest wrongdoers, Parker said, enforce the law and all this would decline.

Would it? Well, lynchings were common in the United States of Parker's day; but there were only three within his jurisdiction during his twenty-one years on the Federal bench.

In taking his oath of office Parker swore to "administer justice without respect to persons, and do equal rights to the rich and poor." To this pledge of impartial honesty he added the practice of efficiency. Fairness was not enough along the border—speed was needed too. Only by quick action could a judge impress frontiersmen and clear up the accumulating cases.

Parker found that out at once. The Arkansas part of his district was easily handled. There, state and county courts had most of the headaches; Parker came into the picture only now and then, as when an Ozark moonshiner was caught for selling liquor without paying Federal tax. But to the west, in the seventy thousand square miles of Indian country, there were neither state nor county judges. Tribal courts took care of matters involving Indians alone. All other cases, civil and criminal alike, went to Fort Smith.[1]

---

[1] As the Indian Territory grew in population, the Fort Smith court was unable to handle all the work. In 1883, therefore, part of the Indian country was assigned to Federal courts in Kansas and Texas. After 1889 the less-important cases could be tried by new courts out in the Indian country. Con-

Nothing daunted, Parker buckled down to work and kept on working till he died. On May 10, 1875, the day he took the oath, the Judge also charged the grand jury and took up eleven cases, involving an estate, liquor offenses, assaults with intent to kill, a jail break, larceny and murder. That was a fair sample of what was to come. In the first term, which ran until the end of June, Parker presided over a dozen-and-a-half murder trials, all but three of which ended with convictions for murder or manslaughter.

Year by year the totals mounted. Sessions often started at seven-thirty in the morning, ran until noon, then from one-thirty until six, with an occasional night session lasting as late as eleven. This went on six days a week, and Parker ran one term into another, keeping court in session nearly all the time. (It was 291 days in the typical year of 1882-83, 116 of these being given to murder trials.) According to the local press, Parker's was the "hardest worked court in all the wide realm of the United States, and it is a subject of universal wonder ... how the court officials, especially the Judge and District Attorney, hold out under such unremitting, complicated and arduous labors."

Statistics tell the story. Parker disposed of more than six hundred cases annually. Twice, in 1890-91 and again two years later, he went over the thousand mark. His grand total was 13,500, of which 1,500 were civil and 12,000 criminal cases.

---

gress later increased the power of the courts on the ground, and on September 1, 1896, Parker's jurisdiction over territory west of Arkansas came to an end.

Seventeen hundred of the criminal cases were dropped by the government. The rest were pressed to a conclusion and yielded 8,600 convictions (by jury trial and pleas of guilty) as against 1,700 verdicts of acquittal. A score, in other words, of 5 to 1.

The cases ran the gamut of frontier crime. Look at the year Belle Starr was tried, 1882-83. As usual, liquor offenses led the list—bootlegging and tax evasion. Next in number came assaults with intent to kill. Then cases of contempt of court, in which Parker cracked down on lying witnesses. Murder was in fourth place that year, with twenty cases to the juries and only seven acquittals. Also on the docket were cases of larceny, rape, forgery, arson, perjury, intimidating witnesses, cutting timber on government land, resisting arrest, filing fraudulent claims against the government, receiving stolen goods, passing counterfeit money, and robbing the mails. Quite a region, the frontier.

It was logical that the murder cases should attract the most attention. Some of the court's partisans regretted this, and pointed out that Judge Parker handled four times as many civil suits as he did murder cases. And in the court's criminal work, killers were outnumbered ten to one by whisky peddlers.

Judge Parker did not argue thus. He knew and boasted that his first concern was murder. In many years a third of his court days were taken up with murder trials. Further time was given to assaults with intent to kill. Liquor cases took time, too; but, after all, illicit-whisky peddling was important chiefly because it set the stage for crimes of violence.

As for civil suits, the Hanging Judge was little interested in these. So he said publicly at the end of his career, sneering at those who prized their houses more than their heart's blood.

"Avarice, which is the curse of the age," he said in his aggressive way, "has so poisoned the people that civil law for the protection of property concerns it more than the criminal law which protects life."

Yes, he was a hanging judge, and he was proud of it. His court tried more than three hundred men and women on the charge of murder. Some were acquitted; some were convicted of manslaughter. One hundred and sixty-four, in Parker's time, were held guilty of murder by juries of their peers. One of these was shot while trying to escape. A second died in jail while awaiting sentence,[1] and two others were quickly given new trials, in which they won acquittal. All the rest, four women and one hundred and fifty-six men, were sentenced by Judge Parker to be hanged by the neck until dead. Pardons, commutations and new trials cut this staggering total in half, but seventy-nine paid the final penalty on Hangman Maledon's gallows.

Speaking of these seventy-nine, Judge E. E. Bryant said that their fate served as an effective warning to the Southwest frontier.

"No court," he said, "has ever wielded a more salutary influence over a semi-civilized country filled with the worst of criminals."

"A man less resolute would have failed," added Colonel Ben T. DuVal, who had grown up with the

---

[1] Two others died in jail after being sentenced, while awaiting execution. Apparently the Western bad men were not so rugged after all.

border country. "A failure would have meant blood-
shed and a fierce domination of the lawless class."

"We are proud of the record of the court at Fort
Smith," said Parker, simply, "We believe we have
checked the flood of crime."

To hang his killers, Isaac Parker went beyond the
functions of an ordinary judge. As was customary, he
presided, checked court accounts, instructed grand
and petit juries, and handed out the sentences. Had he
stopped there he might have sent two dozen to their
doom in his twenty-one years in Fort Smith.

But to Parker that was not enough. There was
pandemonium in the Indian country, there was need
to terrify the border bandits, to shock the men of
blood into dread of the law. The Hanging Judge
therefore chose to aid the marshals who rounded up
the bad men. He helped the district attorneys prosecute the murderers; he steered the jurors toward the
death verdict.

There are ways of cracking down on judges who
usurp non-judicial powers. But Isaac Parker stood
his ground almost to the end. He counted on the
public to support him. He counted on his politician-
friends. He counted on the amazing legal status of
his court.

The public backing was substantial. Citizens of
Fort Smith were more concerned about results than
about legal niceties. Parker's predecessor had been
weak and vicious; Parker was strong and incorruptible. Was that not enough? Why worry if His Honor
took over some of the duties of prosecutor and jury?
Was it not all in the cause of justice?

So with the people to the west. Although the Indian Territory was "steeped in crime and stained with gore," decent citizens were in the great majority. The trouble came from a minority of lawbreakers, many of them fugitives from the justice of several states. By disposing of such characters, Parker won the favor of many honest people, Indian, white, and Negro. And if the Judge was sometimes more than judge, that merely served to keep wrongdoers from escaping the punishment that they deserved.

The Department of Justice also let Parker run things as he pleased. Before 1875 the Fort Smith court had functioned badly, causing the Department every sort of difficulty. Under Parker things went smoothly. To be sure, the Hanging Judge's methods were irregular, but he was efficient. His aim, moreover, was the same as that of the Attorney General—to secure convictions.

Politics helped, too. Parker's Republican party ran the show in Washington during the Judge's first decade on the bench. Parker thus had good contacts and could influence appointments in his district. As a judge, he was reluctant to mix in such matters; but as he said, "it is material to me that these men should be honest and competent." In consequence, he used his influence to secure and retain the services of such men as United States Marshal D. P. Upham, "the man of all others" for this job. Upham was "as fine a man as ever I saw," Parker wrote the White House, adding that the marshal was honored by all "except Ku Klux, thieves, cutthroats, gamblers, drunkards and . . . liars."

There was one bad slip—in 1880 President Rutherford B. Hayes gave the marshal's job to Valentine Dell. Parker considered Dell "ill natured, irascible impractical and tyranical," a friend of "bad and reckless men who want an opportunity to filch money from the government." His Honor therefore set out to get Dell's scalp.

"While we had the strong arm of an able and honest, and effective Marshal to protect us we could enforce the law and make its power felt . . ." he wrote Hayes, "In the interest of justice and right . . . peace and security . . . send me a man here as Marshal who can and will do his duty."

In this fight Judge Parker had the aid of his district attorney, William H. H. Clayton, and of that prosecutor's brother, Powell Clayton, the Republican boss of Arkansas. That made a strong combination; and Dell was dropped early in 1882.

Besides his public and political connections, Parker was aided by the lack of precedents and by the strange fact that for fourteen years he had authority to pronounce sentences from which there was no appeal to any other court.

It is not surprising that there should have been few precedents. Under the Constitution of the United States, ordinary criminal jurisdiction rests with the states rather than with the national government. By Parker's time state legislatures had passed many laws, and state judges had rendered all sorts of decisions on homicide. The United States, by contrast, had few laws and decisions in this field. This left Parker almost on his own when he was handling murder cases. He could, but did not need to, follow the rules of state courts. He was expected to respect the old English common law, but that was fuzzy and ambiguous and could be interpreted in many ways.

And there was no appeal. During two-thirds of his reign Judge Parker could disregard or twist custom in criminal cases without running the risk of being reversed by a higher court. This was owing to a technicality, an oversight of law. In trying murder cases, Parker's Fort Smith tribunal functioned as a circuit court, and the statutes covering such trials failed to provide any means of taking appeals to the Supreme Court of the United States. Under the pardoning power, the President could cancel or change a Parker sentence, but until 1889 no court could challenge the authority of the Hanging Judge in criminal cases.

To some this smacked of tyranny.

"Shall the power of judges exceed that of the Russian Czar?" asked one editor, "and is there any country on earth even one half civilized that gives the power to commit judicial murder without chance or hope of appeal?"

Isaac Parker made no answer until after 1889. Then, when appeals were allowed in important cases, he spoke out against the new departure.

Supreme Court justices, he said, were learned in the civil, not the criminal law. That being so, they would "look to the shadow in the shape of technicalities instead of the substance in the form of crime."

"The appellate court exists mainly to stab the trial judge in the back," ran one of his last statements on the subject, "and enable the criminal to go free."

In saying that Parker was looking back upon his own career. He, for sure, had never made "hair splitting distinctions in favor of the criminal at the expense of life." Rather he had brushed aside the legal technicalities and had thrown his whole weight against the men of blood.

Was that lynch law? Was that a drumhead spirit?

No, said Parker, he had given every prisoner a chance to prove his innocence. But he had also been determined to let no guilty person escape fitting punishment. His aim had been "to cause bad men to fear the law and good men to respect it . . . None are so high in station as to be above it, and none so low as to be beyond it . . . As does the light of Heaven, it blesses rich and poor alike, and if enforced without fear, favor or affection . . . every man can feel that there is none to molest him, or make him afraid."

CHAPTER FOUR

It Took Brave Men

*Being a U. S. Marshal may appear to some to be a
regular picnic, but we don't want any of it.*

—Fort Smith Elevator, 1884

Have been in pursuit of Little Buck five days," wrote
Captain L. W. Marks from a tiny town in the Osage
country in 1881. "Run on him today. He, with five
others showed fight, resulting in the killing of Little
Buck. Indians reported in gangs waiting for me to
pull out. I am compelled to wait a day or two for
excitement to subside."

So read a routine report from one of the men who
rode for Parker—a deputy marshal of the United
States court in Fort Smith. There were no flourishes,
no dramatics. The deputies were simple men and
expected danger as a part of each day's work.

Captain Marks, an Indian, was a veteran deputy,
well known on the frontier. He held a warrant for
the arrest of Little Buck, an Osage horse thief. Determined not to face Judge Parker, Little Buck had
boasted that he would kill anyone who tried to take

64

him to Fort Smith for trial. Sure enough, Captain Mark's one-man posse, E. M. Mathews, had been found dead one morning, full of bullet holes.

Swearing in another aide, Deputy Marks continued his pursuit and was lucky enough to catch Little Buck some distance from his gun. The young Osage was surrounded by his friends; but the marshal and his assistant had the whole half-dozen covered.

He was an officer, Marks called out in the Osage tongue. He had a writ from the Fort Smith court. Would Little Buck come in without an argument?

Yes, the horse thief grumbled, he couldn't fight without his gun.

So far, so good; but as Marks' posse brought out the handcuffs, Little Buck reached for his knife.

Even then Captain Marks held fire. Arrest meant a two-dollar fee, plus double mileage back to Fort Smith. The latter item would not be collectible if the prisoner were dead. Besides, the deputy might lose his job because of reckless shooting.[1]

"Halt!" cried Marks, "drop the knife!"

But Little Buck came on, and Marks brought him down, with a bullet in the thigh.

The intention was to wound, not kill; but Little Buck died that night. And Marks was in the country of the dead man's friends. So the officer decided to lie quiet for a while in the little village of Pawhaska. When the excitement blew over he slipped off to Fort Smith, taking along two horse thieves, Buffalo Face and John Possue. For these the Captain drew the

---

[1] In 1896 Parker sentenced Deputy Marshal Bee Mellon to three years in the penitentiary because "shooting in an attempt to make an arrest must be better justified than it was when he committed his offense."

usual fees, and Judge Parker gave each a penitentiary sentence.

That was one trip of one deputy marshal. In the days of the Hanging Judge the Fort Smith court had from a hundred to two hundred deputy marshals at a time, and many of them made a half-dozen trips each year.

They were not supermen, these deputies. They were ordinary workaday mortals of average intellect and less-than-average education. They took their jobs for pay rather than for adventure, more to feed their families than to serve the cause of justice. But without them Isaac Parker could not have held court for a single day.

No one knew this better than did Parker, who missed no chance to praise the "judicious, proper, faithful" deputies. "Without these officers," he said more than once, "what is the use of this court?" And when he talked about his record on the bench, the Fort Smith judge never forgot to give much of the credit to the marshal's force, especially the sixty-five who were killed in line of duty.

"It takes men who are brave," he said, "to uphold the law here."

Sad to say, the bravery was bought at bargain rates. Being without fixed salaries, the men who rode for Parker had to rely on fees, mileage, and such rewards as came their way. Everything considered, deputies did not average five hundred dollars a year. While the more active and successful ran well above this figure, their totals were not net income. A quarter of all fees and mileage went to the chief marshal. Travelling expenses cut into what was left, and it was often necessary to buy information and to split with volunteer assistants.

At first glance, the schedule of payments did not seem bad for the nineteenth century (with eggs at a dime a dozen and all that). Mileage was allowed at six cents a mile when the officer was going out from Fort Smith on official business. If he brought back a prisoner, he could claim ten cents a mile for himself on the return trip, plus an equal amount for his captive. Fifty cents was the normal fee for serving papers, two dollars for making an arrest. A deputy could also claim expenses at not to exceed a dollar a day for time spent in chasing criminals.

But look a little closer, at a deputy sent a hundred miles to get two witnesses. If the witnesses could not be located, the officer received nothing at all—neither fees nor mileage. A successful trip meant six-cent miles, one way only, fifty cents for contacting the first witness, thirty-seven cents the second. This would make $6.87 or, after deducting the head marshal's share, $5.15,—eighty-five cents less than the round-trip train fare. A mounted or walking deputy could clear something on the deal but he would have precious little to show for his time.

If the deputy had no money in the bank (few did) his situation was still worse. The government never paid ahead of time and was often six months or a year behind. Hard-pressed deputies had to dispose of their accounts to speculators at such a discount that the $5.15 would drop to about $4.50.

The system worked no better for deputies who were

killers. Officers were paid as much for
small-time whisky peddlers as for capturing
e outlaws. It was two dollars either way, even
if the taking of a murderer had meant a long pursuit,
the raising of a posse and a bloody fight.

In theory there was a dollar a day in expense money
for a deputy who was tracking down a slayer. But to
collect that sum the officer had to present vouchers and
receipts in perfect order. This was rarely possible,
for, as Parker's grand jury said in 1894, "a traveler
would meet with less difficulties to obtain receipts or
vouchers in the English language among the Hotten-
tots or Eskimos than in the majority of route localities
in the Indian Territory."

The government of the United States sometimes put
up rewards for criminals, as in cases of mail robbery
and the murder of Federal employees. Deputies, however, could not share in these rewards, since they were
already being paid by the United States to catch lawbreakers. There was much grumbling at this rule, and
little wonder, for the rewards often totalled five hundred dollars, as against a ten- to fifty-dollar fee-and-
mileage deal.[1]

It took shooting to catch killers. But the law was
no help there. If he killed a criminal while making an
arrest, the deputy marshal lost the twenty cents a mile
for his trip back to Fort Smith and forfeited whatever
claim he might have had to the dollar a day for expenses prior to the gun fight. Nor could the officer
leave corpses stretched out on the ground, as is done in

---

[1] Deputy marshals could and did receive rewards offered by state and
local governments, by railroad and express companies, and by private individuals.

Wild West movies. If he could not persuade one of the dead man's friends or relatives to haul away the body, the deputy had to take care of the burial himself, and foot the bill.

Suppose the fight went wrong. During Parker's years upon the bench, two dozen deputy marshals operating out of Fort Smith were slain in Indian country. So were twoscore others, hired as guards or posse, making at least sixty-five in all. More than triple that number were wounded badly when on business of the Parker court, many being maimed for life.

What happened then? The grand jury of the United States Court in Fort Smith put it in a nutshell when it said "the Government . . . pays no attention at all to him or his family." There was no allowance for medical fees, none for disability or burial, and nothing for the widow.

Knowing this to be unjust, Isaac Parker called for changes in the system.

"The services of reliable, efficient, trustworthy, intelligent and brave men are indispensable," said grand jurors instructed by the Hanging Judge, "and . . . to secure such services the pay therefor must be . . . adequate."

Not that the setup was bad everywhere. The Fort Smith critics considered the emoluments all right for well-settled areas which had good transportation networks and a population that was reasonably cooperative:

but the conditions of the Indian country are exactly the reverse . . . The facilities for transportation . . . are meager and primitive.

The country is sparsely settled, and the deputy can not rely upon assistance from anyone. The Indian people ... are neither bad nor vicious ... They are, however, from nature, uncommunicative and averse to report and prosecute crimes. This disposition is augmented by fear of bodily injury and death at the hands of criminals.

The result was that the man who rode for Parker had a tough time. Unlike deputies elsewhere, he could seldom travel pleasantly by train, staying at hotels and patronizing restaurants. Instead he had to go on horseback or on foot, which cut his mileage income. And often he travelled for days with little food and was forced to sleep under the stars "with his saddle for a pillow."

It was that way in 1875, when the Parkers went to the Southwest; and despite appeals to Washington there was little change in the next two decades. No wonder scores of deputies quit in disgust, to become farmers, or country storekeepers, or detectives for express and railroad companies. The odd thing is that so many stayed so long.

A few of Parker's deputies turned into bandits—the famous Dalton brothers, for example. But these were the exception, not the rule. Most officers served faithfully and well, and continued to respect the law after they had turned in their commissions.

Not that they were angels. Some were bullies. Some were ingrates. Nearly all were cursing and unsentimental individuals inclined to disregard the rights of others. But they did get results. They served the cause of justice on the frontier.

The *Fort Smith Elevator* said this pretty well on Christmas Day in 1885. It was necessary in that issue to announce the death of Deputy Marshal Dave Layman, who had been slain while he was bringing in a batch of prisoners for trial.

"Layman was rather a tough character," admitted the editor of the *Elevator*, "but was one of the bravest and most daring officers that ever traversed the Indian country in quest of criminals."

That Dave had faults none could deny. He was a vulgar loudmouthed braggart with a taste for low women—sometimes he took a harlot along when he was on official business. Dave was mean, too, and his enemies claimed that he made a practice of building-up "very frivolous cases" for the fees. ("Shame on the Government!" screamed the critics when trivial arrests were made. "It is bringing the authority of the U. S. into contempt.")

In all probability the charges against Deputy Layman were correct. But Dave had another side. He had the character and integrity to spurn bribes offered by illicit-liquor dealers and others anxious to evade the law. Besides, he was absolutely fearless when tracking down a killer. And while he often acted with brutality, his death came from an act of kindness. When headed toward Fort Smith with three captives he allowed one of his prisoners to attend a wedding. This made possible a general break and in the mix-up Dave was killed.

Had there been no wedding Layman might have lasted long enough to match the records of the most famous Parker deputies, Heck Thomas, Heck Bruner, and Captain J. H. Mershon. But even as it was, Dave lasted longer than did many others.

Quite a few died at the very start, when they were being broken in as officers. One of these was William Hardin, shot down by bootleggers while on his second trip as deputy. Another was Henry Miller, the guard who did not realize that his prisoner could reach the ax. Another, the young Delaware Indian who was tempted by the five dollars offered to anyone who would help Deputy Marshal J. C. Wilkerson round up liquor smugglers. And still another, overconfident John Carleton, a newly commissioned officer who thought he could catch a hardened criminal without swearing in a posse.

Others of the slain were veterans, experienced marshals who had long since proved their courage, coolness, and marksmanship. Some were careless, some outnumbered, some just unlucky.

Take Willard Ayers, a rough-and-ready deputy of the Dave Layman type. In 1880 Ayers had been nine years an officer of the Fort Smith court and had often demonstrated his skill and resourcefulness.

Ayers was on a routine job, rounding up Emmanuel Patterson, who was wanted on a charge of larceny. Being expert at the business, the deputy located his man and moved in to make the arrest.

"Open up!" he cried, pounding on the door of the house where Patterson was staying, "Open up, God damn you."

It was just routine. Ayers had said those words many times before in his nine years as deputy. But Emmanuel Patterson was scared or nervous, and he shot Willard Ayers through the door.

As was the custom in such cases, the United States

Government put up a reward for the capture of the killer. So did the dead man's brother. Nevertheless it was eight years before the murderer was taken into custody. In 1888 Patterson surrendered to one of Parker's famous deputies, Heck Thomas. After Heck brought him in for trial a Fort Smith jury, brushing aside a plea of self-defense, decided on a verdict of "guilty of murder." Judge Parker sentenced the slayer to die upon the gallows. President Grover Cleveland, however, changed this to life imprisonment on the ground that the evidence was "not . . . of that satisfactory character that would justify the infliction of the death penalty."

Another veteran killed in line of duty was the popular and friendly Addison Beck. Beck was a family man who used his marshal's fees to support his wife and three small children. Unlike Dave Layman and Willard Ayers, he was a peaceful, gentle person. He was efficient, too, one of the most dependable of deputies. The early eighties saw him bringing in a steady stream of candidates for Parker justice, as many as eleven at a time. Then, in January, 1883, he and his posse, Lewis Merritt, went after a sordid ruffian named John Bart. Neither officer came back alive.

Beck's death was only partially avenged. Ten of his friends went out and picked up Johnson Jacks, who had been wounded while helping Bart dispose of the two officers. Jacks died after his capture, before he could be put on trial. Bart, though, got away; and Jacks' death was little comfort to the now-destitute Beck family.

It was cold-blooded murder in the case of the well-known deputy William Irwin. A widower with two children, Irwin had been a mail carrier before he had decided to try his hand at law enforcement. He had become a top-flight officer, cool, quick, and entirely fearless.

Irwin's bravery is seen in one of his last arrests, that of "Judge" James Shanks. Shanks, of course, was not a judge at all; he was a dealer in bootleg whisky. He had some with him in March, 1886, when he was accosted by Deputy Marshal Irwin.

All in all, the "Judge" thought it wise to jump on his horse and make a bid for freedom.

Taking chase, Irwin caught Shanks a half-mile down the road. Both held their fire till the very end; then they exchanged shots at close range. They were so close that there were powder burns from Shanks' pistol on Irwin's hat and hand. But it was the "Judge" who fell, with a bullet in his thigh.

Out on the frontier such wounds often meant blood poisoning and death. Shanks, however, pulled through and faced the real judge. Two hundred dollars, ruled Isaac Parker, and two years in the penitentiary.

Deputy Marshal William Irwin would have been pleased to hear Judge Parker pronounce that sentence. But Irwin was not there to listen; when the Shanks case was called in Fort Smith, Irwin was lying dead out in the wild country to the west. He had been shot from ambush by two members of the Felix Griffin gang.

The final chapter in the Irwin story was written just a month after the deputy had captured Shanks. Irwin ran into the rustler Griffin, arrested him without much difficulty, and started back to Fort Smith with his prisoner. This meant riding through unsettled territory. Two of Griffin's men, Frank Palmer and Jack Spaniard, had concealed themselves along the way. They shot Irwin in the back as he passed by.

The sequel? Frank Palmer managed to escape, and was seen no more in Parker's jurisdiction. Felix Griffin was rearrested, released on bail, and killed while stealing horses. Jack Spaniard was taken prisoner in 1888. He laughed about it, said he did not like to be caged up like a mockingbird. But caged he was, for fourteen months, until he was hanged on the Fort Smith gallows by Judge Parker's direction.

Aware of the dangers of their calling, the men who rode for Parker did what they could to reduce the risks. They planned arrests with care, tried to surprise criminals and demand surrender before the outlaws could reach their weapons. Nor would the officers seek trouble unless they were reasonably sure that they were superior both in numbers and in fire power.

Heck Bruner's fight with Ned Christie illustrates the point. Heck was not a coward. Quite the reverse. It was he who trailed and killed Waco Hampton after that desperado had murdered two deputy marshals and had boasted that he would shoot others "just to see their blood run." Heck, however, was a sensible man who cared more for his life than for vainglorious gestures. He therefore chose to take no foolish chances when, in the fall of 1892, he and two other deputies were asked to bring in the far-famed Christie.

As Bruner knew, Ned Christie was a rough customer, one of the most dangerous outlaws in the border country. A full-blooded Cherokee, Christie had once served in his tribe's legislature, only to turn to the more exciting life of bandit, horse thief, rum-runner, and killer. By the nineties he had killed one Parker deputy, the likeable Dan Maples, and had wounded several others. A posse working under two crack officers, L. P. Isabel and Heck Thomas, cornered Ned in 1889 and shot him in the face. Yet the outlaw managed to escape, and, in getting away, permanently crippled Isabel with a shot through the shoulder.

Heck Bruner, who had chased Christie before, knew that the Cherokee was not to be surprised. Always expecting trouble, Ned holed up with his women and his gang in a log fort near Tahlequah. Nor could the marshals risk an even fight. Christie was a trained gunsmith and marksmen, knew and used guns expertly.

In getting ready, the Fort Smith officers stocked up on rifles, revolvers, and small-arms ammunition. They added a supply of dynamite, and Bruner, with Deputy Paden Tolbert, went to Kansas and borrowed a United States Army cannon that would fire three-pound shells. Meantime Captain G. S. White, a third deputy, raised a posse of ten tested fighting men.

This expeditionary force caught Ned Christie with only two supporters. Even so, the struggle lasted twenty hours. The first two thousand rifle bullets did a minimum of damage—a commentary on frontier marksmanship—and the Christie stronghold quivered but held up under thirty rounds of artillery fire.

The attacking party then used its dynamite. This did the trick; it raised the fort from its foundations and ripped off one whole side. Christie, though he came out fighting, seemed to know that his end was near. His final shots went very wild, and as he stumbled toward the besieging force he was pumped full of lead.

Plan as they might the Parker officers were always running into emergencies. Take the case of Captain Sam Sixkiller, one of the ablest Indian deputies on Parker's staff. Captain Sam and his two assistants were looking around for a couple of petty criminals when, in June, 1895, they ran into most of the Dick Glass gang. Though no Ned Christie, Glass was a troublesome sort of character; and on this occasion he and his friends had the law outnumbered. But when the dust had cleared, Glass and his man Jim Johnson were lying dead upon the ground, and the rest of the outlaws were Captain Sam Sixkiller's prisoners.

It had been the other way around in May, 1885, when Deputy Marshal Jim Guy led a posse of thirteen against the Jim Lee—Tom Pink crowd. With less than half Guy's numbers, the wanted men had routed the officers, killing the deputy and three of his men. Lee and Pink were shot down later by Heck Thomas and another officer, but that did not wipe out the recollection of the heaviest loss sustained by the government in the Indian country in the era of Judge Parker. (There had been an even bloodier day back in the pre-Parker period, when, in 1872, eight officers and five of their opponents had perished as a result of one shooting affray.)

Yes, it was a rugged business, riding for Judge Parker. It was tough to find the criminals, tough to capture them, tough to take them in for trial. A trip paid well if the deputy picked up a reward from an express company or a private party. There was profit, too, when an officer had a large batch of prisoners—Heck Thomas and his posse brought in thirty-two at once in 1887. But four was a more normal load, and more often than not there was no special reward. Just the fees and mileage. And sometimes deputies came in wounded, or did not come in at all.

Even those who remained whole must have suffered from the strain. Note, for instance, the career of Captain J. H. Mershon.

Mershon was perhaps the most efficient of the men who rode for Parker. An active deputy from the seventies until the nineties, he was known as a good subordinate, a good partner, a good leader. He rode well and fought well. He became expert at finding criminals, unearthing evidence, gathering testimony. He learned all there was to learn about the Southwest frontier and its people. He appeared to have some sort of magic that protected him from outlaws' bullets, and he seemed not to worry in the least about the dangers of his trade.

In 1898 Captain Mershon went insane.

CHAPTER FIVE

The Daltons Are Remembered

Their boasted bravery was ... born of a spirit of desperation and pampered into undue proportions for illegitimate purpose. Under the ordinary circumstances of everyday life ... they ... would be found wanting.

> —David Elliot of Coffeyville,
> Kansas, where the Daltons came
> to the end of their trail

Who has heard of Captain Mershon, or Sam Sixkiller, or Heck Bruner, or Tyner Hughes, or Heck Thomas, or Addison Beck, or William Irwin? They were honest, decent deputy marshals who labored on the side of justice—and they are forgotten.

Everybody, though, knows about Bob, Grat, and Emmett Dalton. They, too, were Parker officers; but they quit to become outlaws.

It is natural that the Dalton boys should have picked up some publicity. Their shift of sides was quick and spectacular. On top of that, the brothers are interesting because they represent both the old and new in criminal trends along the border. They were horse thieves at the start, held up trains next, and ended as bank robbers.

This of course is sure fire on the newsstands, in the bookstores, on the air, and in the movies. It is entertaining. It might also be instructive, if the tales bore some resemblance to what really happened. But as time slips by the tendency is to use soft music. Misdeeds are excused, endearing qualities are stressed; and it is suggested that the Daltons were sinned against more than they sinned. The Daltons are then set up as heroes of the old frontier.

In praising the lawbreaking Daltons, the legend makers often fail to note that there was one real hero in the Dalton family. This was Frank, a brother of the famous Bob, Grat, and Emmett. Frank was one of Judge Parker's fighting deputy marshals and was shot down in an effort to bring in the last members of the Felix Griffin gang.

Altogether there were more than a dozen Dalton children. Their father, Louis Dalton, was a Kentuckian, a law-abiding veteran of the war with Mexico. Like Isaac Parker, he moved west into Missouri, where he took a bride. The Daltons' numerous children were born on a farm near Independence, Missouri.

It was tough sledding for the family, for Louis, the father, was no world beater as a farmer. He had some success with horses, and took part in county fairs in Missouri. He died on his way home from one of these, in 1890, before his sons Bob, Grat, and Emmett had made the family name notorious. But even before Louis Dalton's death, his children had begun to scatter.

Some went as far as California. The greater number, however, became associated with various parts of the Indian Territory.

It was Mrs. Louis Dalton who intrigues the legend builders. Adeline Younger was her maiden name; and her half-brother was father of the Younger boys, Cole, Bob, and Jim.

Starting with this link, the frontier storytellers can connect the Daltons with many of the big names of border banditry. The Youngers learned the business from the worst cutthroat of all, William C. Quantrill; and they teamed up with other Quantrill pupils, Frank and Jesse James. The fabulous Belle Starr was one of Cole Younger's mistresses. Belle had a child by Younger—well, anyway, she said Cole was the father. She had another by Jim Reed, a partner of Dan Evans, one of the first six hanged by Isaac Parker. Later, Belle teamed up with Sam Starr. She and Sam associated with what became the Felix Griffin gang; and a member of the Griffin gang killed Frank Dalton. To round things out, Sam's nephew, Henry Starr, later shot and killed Bob Dalton's former partner, Floyd Wilson.

Such ties delight a good many people who collect frontier lore. Could there have been a combination of outlaw gangs, a secret brotherhood, a fellowship of desperadoes held together by blood ties and camaraderie?

No, there could not. The links are pretty weak. By similar relationships we could connect the Dalton boys with many of the better people of the Southwest.

Note also that the Younger brothers are the key

to the whole pattern. These boys have been provided with the romance-treatment of the sentimentalists; they have emerged as dashing outlaws, entirely capable of being central figures in a grand frontier combine of bad men. But in reality Cole, Bob and Jim were rather inefficient. They showed less than genius in their attempt to rob a Northfield, Minnesota, bank in 1876. The famous James boys were partners in that venture, but all three Youngers were arrested and drew penitentiary terms. By luck, Frank and Jesse James managed to get away.

This happened long before the Dalton brothers rode. No doubt the Daltons knew about the exploits that had put their half-cousins behind bars. But the connection probably ended there. Adeline Younger Dalton bore little resemblance to her outlaw nephews; she tried to raise her children to be good citizens.

Most of them were. When Bob, Grat, and Emmett Dalton were ranking public enemies, brothers and sisters were living uneventful lives in farm communities. And in 1887 one of Mrs. Dalton's boys died fighting on the side of law and order.

In an appraisal of Adeline Younger Dalton and her upbringing of her children, Frank belongs on the credit side. He was a typical frontiersman, foul-mouthed and poorly educated; but he had the strength of character to line up against the outlaws.

In the fall of 1887 Frank Dalton was working the Cherokee Nation with another expert deputy marshal, James Cole. Frank, then in his upper twenties, was one of Judge Parker's veteran officers. He and Cole were on the lookout for bad men in general, and for

Dick Smith in particular. A cattle thief and a boot-legger, Smith was thought to be one of the last survivors of the Felix Griffin gang, which had disposed of Deputy Marshal William Irwin two years before.

When they ran into Smith the Parker officers found the bandit armed and waiting. Dick was backed up by Lee Dixon, his brother-in-law, and by his boarder William Towerly.

"Don't shoot!" yelled Deputy Frank Dalton, "We want no trouble here!"

But Smith did shoot. Dalton fell and lay twisting on the ground, moaning that he was dying. William Towerly then came out and finished him with a bullet through the head.

Meanwhile Smith, Dixon, and Mrs. Dixon were giving their attention to Deputy Cole. But Cole was the lucky sort. A year before, he had killed a drunken bully in a ferryboat brawl, and just before starting after Dick Smith he had survived a clash with a Cherokee bad man, Big Chewee. This time Deputy Cole was wounded, by a shot from Dixon's rifle. But, firing fast, he killed Dick Smith, killed Mrs. Dixon and crippled Dixon, whom he then claimed as his prisoner. Towerly escaped into the Choctaw country, where he and Deputy Marshal Ed Stockery killed each other in a gun fight. Dixon, after apparently recovering from his wound, died of "the fever."

When Frank Dalton was killed, his brother Grat was twenty-six years old, Bob was seventeen, and Emmett only fifteen. It is conceivable that if Frank Dalton had lived he might have kept these brothers from becoming criminals. Whatever his deficiencies,

Frank did have some qualities of leadership. He could steer his brother Grat, who was pugnacious, yet quite willing to let others do the thinking. He also had the admiration of Bob and might have influenced him, though Bob was willful, reckless, and impetuous, and liked to be the leader. If Frank had stayed alive, he might have led Emmett, too, but as it was, Emmett fell under Bob's spell.

One must be careful in dealing with the "ifs" of history. Still, it may be observed that Frank Dalton did direct his brothers into the field of law enforcement. While he lived, and for a time thereafter, Grat, Bob, and Emmett Dalton all rode for Parker. Though not the best of officers, they did good work and became well known around the Fort Smith court.

Emmett, still a boy, seemed not to have held a commission of his own. Nevertheless he learned the trade by riding with his brothers and spent much time in practicing marksmanship.

Grat Dalton was well regarded during his months in government. To all appearances he was a deputy of the Captain Marks or Addison Beck variety, making up for lack of brilliance by careful and consistent performance. Though he nabbed no famous bad men, he brought in much criminal small fry. He proved himself courageous; he was wounded in line of duty the year after Frank was killed.

Bob, who possessed more fire, had the makings of a first-rate officer. He showed promise before he was eighteen, when he was riding with his brother Frank. Later Bob did well as posse for Deputy Marshal Floyd Wilson and as a deputy in his own right. But he had barely served out his apprenticeship when he turned to a life of crime.

Floyd Wilson and Bob Dalton made a good team. Floyd, headstrong and fearless like Bob, burned with a desire for action. He was later to tangle with the remnant of the Barnett gang, which had shot two Parker officers in a single day. Assisted by Bob Dalton, he brought in such rough characters as Carroll Collier and Bud Maxfield.

In those days most people would have said that Floyd Wilson, rather than Bob Dalton, was the ruffian. Though impulsive, Bob seemed relatively inoffensive, while his partner was known for his hot temper.

"There is too much violence used by some of them," wrote one journalist, citing Floyd Wilson and other deputies, "and they don't hesitate to fire their pistols on very trifling occasions."

A Captain Scott, going a good deal further, called Floyd Wilson's habits "malignant and despicable in the extreme." Men like Wilson, said Scott, caused good citizens to fear the "army of U. S. Deputy Marshals, who, like the plagues of Egypt, scour the Indian Territory and arrest men . . . without writ or warrant."

The Captain may have been a little prejudiced. When approached by Wilson and the Andrew brothers, in January, 1884, Scott had failed to recognize the three as deputies and had put up resistance. For this he had received a brutal beating but had come out whole, which was something for those days.

Such incidents led many people to feel that Floyd Wilson would disgrace the Parker court and come to a bad end. Instead, Floyd improved with the passing years. He took on family responsibilities and became noticeably steadier. Yet he retained his spirit, as is seen in his last adventure, his encounter with the celebrated Henry Starr in 1893.

Having no deputy marshal's commission at the time, Floyd Wilson was acting as posse for H. C. Dickey, who was trailing Henry Starr.

John Keck, meeting the officers on their way to the Indian country, warned Wilson to be careful.

"Some of the Starrs are brave people," Keck said. Henry was among the toughest of the clan. Tougher, maybe, than the late Sam Starr, who had been Belle Starr's Indian husband.

Oh, laughed Floyd Wilson, the "right man" could handle that. He and Dickey would bring in Henry Starr, alive or dead.

As if to prove his valor, Floyd Wilson did not wait for Dickey when he sighted Henry Starr. Riding on ahead, he faced the armed outlaw alone and carried the fight to Starr by firing the first shot. But Wilson's gun jammed. That ended his career.[1]

Floyd Wilson, like Frank Dalton, gave his life for the cause of justice and, like Frank Dalton, he is now forgotten. Instead, the spotlight goes to Bob Dalton, who rode both with his brother Frank and with Floyd Wilson but turned from right to wrong and died as an enemy of mankind.

---

[1] For this and other crimes Henry Starr was arrested out in Colorado and brought back to Fort Smith for trial. Parker was all in favor of a hanging, and did not keep his feelings from the jurors. Conviction followed, and Parker twice sentenced Henry Starr to die on the gallows. That he escaped the noose was owing to the new appeals machinery, and to Judge Parker's death. Starr was finally given a penitentiary sentence, but was pardoned by President Theodore Roosevelt in 1903, because of the "probability that he committed this killing in self-defense."

Bob, Grat, and Emmett Dalton could have been farmers had they so desired, for there was land in the family and more to be had along the Southwest frontier. Or the brothers could have kept on earning marshal's fees as long as they wished. But in either occupation the work was hard and the return was small. A career of crime looked more promising.

It was as simple as all that. The legend makers talk of love affairs and heartless creditors, but the plain, unvarnished truth is that the Dalton boys chose the outlaw life because it seemed easy and rewarding.

While they remained in Parker's jurisdiction the brothers specialized in stealing horses. In midsummer, 1890, gossips in Fort Smith were saying that the Daltons had gone wrong. Those who knew Grat, Bob, and Emmett were inclined to discredit the rumors. Still it seemed wise to call Grat Dalton in for questioning.

Riding in during September, 1890, Grat issued a flat denial. It was all a frame-up, he said bluntly. He and Bob and Emmett and all the other Daltons were absolutely innocent, merely the targets of false accusations by their enemies.

Grat got away that time, because of the lack of evidence and because of his record as an officer. He got away, and was not seen again at Parker's court. But Fort Smith often heard of him and of his brothers. By 1891 the Daltons had shifted from rustling to the more profitable business of robbing trains. They committed most of their crimes in the region where they had served as law-enforcement officers. But once, at least, they operated as far away as California. Their last raid, also, carried them and their accomplices out of Parker's jurisdiction, up to Coffeyville in southern Kansas.

That was in October, 1892. Though daring, the Dalton's plan was stupid—a daylight robbery of two city banks. The boys did get their hands on thirty thousand dollars, but as they tried to make their get-away they were cut off by aroused townspeople. The running fight that followed cost eight men their lives. Four citizens of Coffeyville were killed, and as many members of the Dalton gang—Bob and Grat Dalton, Bill Powers, and Dick Broadwell.

Emmett Dalton, who survived the battle, was given life imprisonment. Had the affair occurred within the Parker jurisdiction, he would almost certainly have been sentenced to the gallows.

So closed the sordid story of the Daltons, unless one adds a postscript for Bill Doolin. Bill was a Texas drifter and bad man, who had thrown in his lot with the Daltons. He and two others had been dropped from the Dalton gang just before the disastrous invasion of Coffeyville. The fearful slaughter of that day should have made him reconsider his program for the future. Doolin, though, was, and proposed to remain, an outlaw. He lost no time in forming a new Bill Doolin gang, which terrorized the Southwest for four years.

Being just a bit luckier than the Dalton brothers, Bill Doolin long eluded all his pursuers. In time, however, the ring began to close around him. The rewards mounted—$250 from the marshal of Judge Parker's court; $225 from Southwest City, Missouri; $300 from the Wells Fargo Express Company; $1,000

from the Atchison, Topeka and Santa Fe Railroad—
$2,575 in all.

That was too much for safety. Besides, the Doolin
gang was breaking up. Two members, Tulsa Jack
and Bitter Creek, were shot out in the Indian Territory. Another, Arkansas Tom Jones, was captured in
Kansas and sent up for fifty years.

Doolin's turn was next.

The end came in the summer of 1896, a few months
before Judge Parker's death. Bothered by a leg wound,
Doolin decided to try the baths at Eureka Springs, an
Ozark resort town developed by Isaac Parker's political side-kick, Powell Clayton.

There Doolin was captured after a fight in a bath-
house. He was then confined in Guthrie, Oklahoma,
but in July, 1896, he and thirteen others broke out of
jail.

This was Bill's last success. Heck Thomas, long an
ace Parker deputy, picked up the Doolin trail in
August and, with a posse of six, closed in on the bandit
at the home of his paramour.

Doolin chose to fight—after all, what had he to
lose? And Deputy Heck Thomas brought him down.

Bill Doolin was only thirty-eight when he was killed.
It was too bad he had lived that long.

Bill Dalton, a brother of Grat, Bob, and Emmett,
rode with Doolin for a while. He, too, died a violent
death, shot down by deputies in the country west of
Arkansas.

CHAPTER SIX

Belle Starr, Horse Thief

*He asked me what I thought about his wife going off
with that man ... He said he just thought she was lying
around with him. He said a good many vulgar things
about her which I will not repeat.*

—John West, reporting a talk
with Belle Starr's husband Sam

Those who glorify the old frontier show great interest in Belle Starr. Her very name suggests romance; she packed guns, had many loves, and was associated with famous outlaws. This was enough to get Belle talked about while she was alive. The tales have grown in the fifty years since her death, and Hollywood has presented the Bandit Queen as a proud, full-bosomed beauty, a lady Robin Hood who fought and died for the lost cause of the Confederacy.

In cold reality Belle Starr was neither Union nor Confederate. She had no conscience and no beauty but was a crude, and ugly, nymphomaniac. In 1883 Judge Isaac Parker sent her to the penitentiary for stealing a horse from a crippled boy.

Though it did not make the big-town papers, Belle Starr's trial created quite a stir along the Southwest border. Female defendants were no novelty in the Fort Smith court, but most of these were dreary wretches hauled in for selling "Choctaw beer" or for being mixed up in what Prosecutor Clayton called "whore house brawls." As a horse thief Belle was something special. In the words of one reporter, "the very idea of a woman being . . .the leader of a band of horse thieves . . . was sufficient to fill the court room."

The word "leader" need not be taken seriously. Belle Starr slept with many outlaws but gave orders to very few. She had no gang, and when she did steal livestock she worked on a small scale. Even there, she fumbled.

When put on trial before Judge Parker, Belle was in her middle thirties. Born Myra Belle Shirley, she had lived in Missouri and Texas as well as in the Indian country. Her friendship with criminals began early. She was mistress to Cole Younger for a while, her daughter Pearl presumably being the offspring of that union. (Belle had great plans for Pearl, but the girl was too much like her mother. She became a prostitute.)

When the law closed in on Cole Younger, Belle married, or otherwise became attached to, another bandit, Jim Reed. A villainous brute, Reed was, for a time, associated with Dan Evans, of Hangman Maledon's first sextette. In 1875, the year that Evans stretched rope in Fort Smith, Reed was slaughtered in a Texas gun fight. Belle was left a "widow" with two children, Pearl Younger and Ed Reed. (Ed followed his father's pattern, and in 1889 was brought before Judge Parker for receiving stolen goods. After a term in the penitentiary he changed his ways. On Judge Parker's recommendation, President Cleveland restored Reed's civil rights, and for a time Ed was a deputy marshal of the Fort Smith court. But he met his death in a drunken brawl in a cheap frontier saloon.)

After Jim Reed's death, Belle moved into the Indian Territory. There she took up with a Cherokee, Sam Starr, calling herself his wife and settling down at Younger's Bend in the Cherokee Nation.

There were good and bad Starrs in the Indian country. Sam and his father were bad Starrs. It was old Tom who told a friend that he had done many bad things in his day but really regretted only one. That was when he had set fire to the house of an enemy. A little boy came running out of the burning building, and Tom Starr tossed him back into the flames.

Tom guessed the Lord would not be likely to forgive him for that.

No, allowed the friend, he guessed not.

Although she took Sam's name, Belle did not intend to restrict her favors to him alone. Among the others on her list was a border drifter by the name of Childs. This Childs, who helped the Starrs with their horse stealing, lived with Belle in the early weeks of 1882, when Sam was at his father's house, "tolerably bad off" with the measles.

The business did not end when Sam got home. He was soon complaining to a neighbor that Belle was "lying around" with Childs. That was the kind of slut she was, said Sam, and he expected she would run off with Childs or some one else some time. Or kill Sam, maybe. Worrying about that, Sam took the precaution of stealing Childs' pistol.

Belle spoke as ill of Sam. At this same time, when another neighbor threatened Starr with arrest, Belle said "she did not care what the hell" was done to Sam. For there were other men. . . .

Inconstant, Belle Starr was also dull-witted. This is evident in the affair that brought her to grief before Judge Parker. In April, 1882, she and Sam stole some horses, taking them from the range near their home at Younger's Bend. The plan was to dispose of the animals down in McAlester. There was profit in it— good stolen horses brought around forty dollars each. But there was risk involved in working so close to home. Both thieves and horses could be recognized with ease.

Thus it was to be. On April 20, 1882, Belle Starr told John West, who lived five miles down the road, that she wanted to "pass some horses." Would he help her pen them?

West, no angel himself, gladly agreed to aid her, apparently expecting a share of the loot. Then he spied a large bay horse with a star on its forehead and a rope mark on its left foreleg. This horse, as John West and Belle Starr both knew, belonged to Andrew Crane, a lame young man who lived near by.

"If I was in your place I would not take the horse . . . " said West, "It belongs to . . . a cripple."

"God damn the horse," snapped Belle Starr, adding

that she didn't "want to steal it." But steal it she did, and that was that.

When he heard of what had happened, Andrew Crane limped over to Younger's Bend, and had a "right smart" talk with Belle. It was a good horse, Andrew said. It was double gaited and worth all of eighty-five dollars. He wanted it back in a hurry, or else the money.

Well, said Belle, Andrew was "a poor boy and a crippled boy." She felt sorry for him. He should go get thirty dollars from John West, and then she would take care of the rest. But Andrew Crane had better watch his step and not talk to the deputy marshals from Fort Smith. ("If I had her and Sam brought down . . ." was Andrew's recollection of Belle's statement, " Sam would not be a bit too good to waylay my road.")

John West, however, would not give Crane the thirty dollars. When the lame boy told West of Belle's suggestion, West cursed and growled that "he'd be damned if he would pay for something he did not get, that they had been trying for some time to get him into something of that kind."

So Andrew tried the Starrs again.

"He ought to be in hell . . ." Belle snorted on hearing what John West had said. "He got forty dollars of the money."

Sam Starr was much more vague. As Andrew Crane remembered it, Sam claimed that while he had not stolen the horse, "he almost knew who took it but . . . he could not swear to it."

That might be, moaned Andrew, but he was out a

horse. Not that he wanted trouble. Just the money. If he got satisfaction he would even leave the neighborhood (it wasn't such a good place anyway) and go out West "to keep down a fuss."

All right, said Belle Starr, she would put up thirty dollars; that would be better than giving it to the "big lawyers" down at Judge Parker's court. She would go down to Muskogee and would send Andrew Crane the bills in a letter, but he "must not claim it as hush money;" she only wanted time to try to find the horse.

Andrew waited quite a while, but he never saw the horse or money. When his father stepped in to help, Belle Starr denounced the senior Crane as a "damned old Arkansas hoosier" who should have "kept his mouth shut." Andrew's brother-in-law got much the same when he went over to Younger's Bend. ("Mrs. Starr came out with a tirade of abuse and said if she ever got out of this she would make it hot for us fellows.")

Finally someone shot at Andrew Crane while he was looking for his horse. So at long last the crippled boy called in the law. He was joined by a Cherokee, Sam Campbell, whose grey mare had been taken by the Starrs.

Warrants were sworn out in July, 1882, and the dependable Captain Marks made the arrests that fall. Belle and Sam Starr came in without a struggle, hoping they could win before the United States commissioner (in the preliminary hearing) or, failing that, in open court. While awaiting trial they secured release on bail. Sam's relatives took care of that, old Tom

Starr listing assets of $5,300 (250 cattle—$3,750; 25 horses—$1,250; 160 sheep—$300). The Starrs also paid for the services of a good law firm, Cravens and Marcum.

The defense attorneys did what they could at the commissioner's hearing (October, 1882) and did their best in a four-day trial before Judge Parker (February, 1883). They worked on citizenship, for one thing—the rule that this court could not touch quarrels between Indians. Belle was clearly under Parker's jurisdiction; despite her alliance with Sam, she was legally "a white woman and not an Indian." But Sam, as a Cherokee, could not be brought into the Campbell case, Campbell also being a red man. Cravens and Marcum pointed out that Crane, too, had Indian blood and perhaps was a citizen of the Cherokee Nation. Crane, however, proved that he was living in the Indian country "as a white people;" and Sam stayed in the picture.

The defense then tried to use Sam's measles to set up an alibi. The horses had been stolen during the third week of April, 1882; and lots of Starrs were ready to swear that Sam was "down sick" from March until the end of May, Belle being at his bedside "most of the time." But this exploded when the prosecution caught the witnesses in contradictions. "I can't exactly keep dates," Sam's aunt confessed, and old Tom Starr did worse than that.

"I don't know what date of the month this is," he admitted under cross-examination, "Indians don't keep the day of the month like white people. We keep it by the moon."

The only chance remaining was to attack John West, the prosecution's key witness. But West was firm and stuck to his story, Judge Parker and Prosecuting Attorney Clayton helping him a little. That sealed the fate of the defendants.

The court was jammed the whole four days, and all eyes were on Belle Starr. Everyone could see that she was a very homely woman, with her thin, long mouth, her hawk-like nose, her large ears and coarse hair, her scrawny frame. She lacked grace of carriage and looked much older than she was.

Belle was lively, though. She refused to take the witness stand. She wrote notes for her attorneys. She cried appropriately when some one mentioned Jim Reed, her former "husband." And while Sam seemed sad and dull, Belle looked up at Isaac Parker with a bold and fearless glance.

It did not help her much. The jury found both Sam and Belle guilty of stealing Andrew Crane's bay horse, and also ruled that Belle had stolen Sam Campbell's mare. This verdict suited the Judge, who then sentenced each of the defendants to one year in the House of Correction in Detroit.

In a way, Belle's sentence was the lighter, for she had been convicted on two counts, and Sam on only one. But it was common sense, not chivalry, that prompted Parker to rule that way. It was clear that Sam and Belle both were guilty on both counts. A technicality of jurisdiction removed Sam Starr from the Campbell case, but there was nothing to prevent the Judge from making all things even in the sentences.

Parker also considered the fact that it was the first conviction for both defendants. So His Honor chose a short term, hoping that Belle and Sam Starr might yet decide to become decent citizens.

It was a misplaced hope. When sentenced, Sam was sullen, Belle defiant. Sullen and defiant they remained when sent on to Detroit. (They travelled with five guards and twenty fellow prisoners, Belle being the only woman in the party of twenty-six.)

Their new home was a model institution, one which had earlier been run by Zebulon Brockway, the greatest warden of his day. Under Brockway's guiding hand, the House of Correction had become just that, a prison stressing education and redemption as well as punishment.[1] But Belle and Sam did not want to be redeemed.

On their release, the pair went back to Younger's Bend and their old ways. They were a little wiser, possibly, for they were not again caught stealing neighbor's horses. But they still harbored outlaws, still led immoral, brawling lives. They were mixed up pretty badly with the horse thief and killer Felix Griffin, and with Griffin's hatchet man, Jack Spaniard (hanged by Parker's order in 1889). Belle now had a love affair with a wretch named John Middleton. He was drowned or shot to death before he could be hanged. Some said Sam Starr killed him out of jealousy, but probably not. By this time Sam was used to sharing Belle.

---

[1] In their year in Detroit, Buffalo Chips and White Bear picked up trades and learned to read and write. Noting their improvement, the *Fort Smith New Era* wrote: "Moral—if you wish to become useful and high toned, steal something and pass one year at the model prison of the world, the House of Correction at Detroit, Michigan."

The Fort Smith court saw a good deal of Belle and Sam in 1886. In January Belle came in to attend the trial of one of her current love interests, a handsome young Indian with an interesting name, Blue Duck. Belle did all she could to help, giving her friend advice and lining up the best of legal talent. If anything, her aid prejudiced the jury. Blue Duck was convicted of murder while his partner was acquitted.

Blue Duck did not hang. He was twice reprieved and then (September, 1886) President Cleveland changed his sentence to life imprisonment "because of some doubt as to his guilt."

According to the Belle Starr fans, Blue Duck was even luckier than that.

"After a year," they say, "through the agency of unseen influences, of which Belle Starr was said to have wielded the directing hand, his pardon was secured and he was set free."

This, of course, sets Belle Starr up as a "fixer," a woman of great brains and power, able to outwit the United States Government and make the White House do her bidding.

There is one catch. Blue Duck did not get a pardon in a year. He was still in prison when Belle Starr died in 1889, and he stayed there six years more. By then he had consumption, and the doctors gave him only one more month to live. The President therefore issued a pardon (March, 1895), "permitting the convict to die among his friends."

Shortly after Blue Duck's trial, Belle Starr herself was arrested by Deputy Marshal Tyner Hughes. Some one shot at Hughes that trip—a not uncommon business out near Younger's Bend. But the officer went on about his work and brought in, not only Belle Starr, but also two suspected killers and five other doubtful characters.

During June, 1886, Belle was examined and discharged in a holdup case. N. H. Farrell, the victim, admitted that she looked smaller than the bandits who had broken into his store.

Anyway, Farrell said sadly, he was "not able to identify anybody. I was robbed. I could not tell if any woman was dressed in man's clothes."

A few weeks after that, Belle successfully fought the charge that she had stolen a horse from one Albert McCarty. ("We the jury find Belle Starr not guilty as charged in the within indictment.") Other cases against Belle were continued and, for lack of satisfactory evidence, were never brought to trial.

Meanwhile Sam Starr was in difficulties, the charge being that he and Felix Griffin had robbed a post office in 1885. The take had been extremely small—little more than pocket change—but Judge Parker's deputies had come to the conclusion that the country west of Arkansas would be better off without either Starr or Griffin.

Sam, who was on the scout, was finally located, shot down and taken prisoner. Despite his wounds he managed to escape. Soon he changed his mind, decided to stand trial and rode into Fort Smith to surrender. So Parker had both Sam Starr and Felix Griffin indicted in the fall of 1886.

The trial was set for March, 1887, but was never held. Sam, out on bail, was killed in a frontier gun fight before March rolled around. And Felix Griffin was shot to death a little later.

Again a "widow," Belle Starr took up with a young Indian outlaw, Jim July—called Jim Starr by Belle's request. Like others of his kind, Jim had trouble with the Parker court. For a time he managed to get his cases continued; then he jumped bail and went on the scout. The deputies tracked him down, wounding him badly in the gun fight that resulted in his capture. While awaiting trial, Jim died in the hospital connected with Judge Parker's jail.

Even so, Jim outlived his ladylove. In February, 1889, Belle Starr died in the mud out near her home, shot in the back by some person still unknown.

CHAPTER SEVEN

Other Ladies of the Court

*If I didn't have to kill him I would not have done it.
I always thought a person had a right to protect themselves.*

—Fannie Echols

Though a thief and an adulteress, Belle Starr was not
a killer. But blood did stain the hands of several other
frontier ladies who showed up in the Parker court.

Most of the female slayers were short on glamor,
and their crimes were not exactly romantic. Take
Polly Ann Reynolds as an illustration. Miss Reynolds,
who weighed two hundred and eighty pounds, was
brought to Fort Smith charged with kicking a friend
to death at a New Year's celebration.

More typical than Polly Ann were the girls brought
to book for disposing of their husbands or lovers.
Judge Parker sentenced four such creatures to the
gallows (none were executed) and sent several others
to the penitentiary.

Mrs. Alvirado Hudson Tucker provides a fairly good
example. For some time Alvirado lived on the frontier

as the wife of a peaceful farmer named John Hudson. Then she became interested in a more exciting man, Bill Tucker. Bill, one of Judge Parker's old acquaintances, had done time in the Detroit House of Correction. It was hard to pin things on Bill, for he was a slippery character; but there was reason to believe that he was a burglar and horse thief, a train robber, bootlegger, and murderer.

Under the circumstances, John Hudson did not stand much chance. Bill Tucker openly boasted that he planned to kill the farmer; and in June, 1887, Hudson was shot from ambush while he was working in his garden. Whereupon his widow married Tucker.

Cold-blooded murder, said the neighbors, and both Tucker and the woman were involved. Judge Parker thought so, too, and spoke publicly of his "well-grounded suspicion." But the evidence was so sketchy that the Fort Smith officers could not build up the case for trial.

Well, then, try something else. If the Tuckers could not be convicted of murder, perhaps they could be sent up on another charge.

Bill being the more likely prospect, the deputies began on him. In January, 1888, he was arrested on a charge of train robbery. When that failed to stick, he was charged with smuggling liquor into the Indian country.

Bill posted bond, left Fort Smith in a hurry, forfeiting his bail and going on the scout. But the deputies, quickly after him, picked him up again on warrants listing counts of robbery and horse stealing.

And while Bill cooled his heels in jail the officers went on accumulating evidence of larceny and murder.

Judging her husband's chances to be pretty poor, Mrs. Tucker decided to help him get out of jail. So, working with two small-time scoundrels, she contacted a trusty, Charles Wilson.

Trusty Wilson, a cagey fellow, indicated that he might be interested. But he then took the news to Jailer Pettigrew.

See it through, the Jailer said, get the saws from Alvirado Tucker. Judge Parker wanted evidence that would convict that female.

Good enough, said Wilson, and went back to see Mrs. Tucker. She handed him the saws, which were taken from him in a prearranged search as soon as he got back to the jail.

Bill Tucker did not make his break. Instead, his wife and her accomplices were taken into custody. For her role in the affair Alvirado Tucker drew a one-year term in the penitentiary. Against her husband the prosecution was able to establish three cases of horse theft and one of burglary; so Bill went up for eleven years.

The Tucker woman, not much to look at, won little sympathy from the residents of Fort Smith. There was much more feeling for Fannie Echols, the first woman sentenced to the gallows by Judge Parker.

Fannie was a bright-looking girl of twenty, a trifle fleshy but neat and attractive. She and John Williams worked for the same employer out in the Creek Nation and, though not married, found it convenient to live together. Fannie was pleased with the arrangement until her friend developed a possessive streak. From then on, it was not so good.

"John was jealous of me," Fannie later testified, "and had been whipping me for a long time." Eventually the girl figured that enough was enough and shot John Williams through the heart.

To hear Fannie tell it, hers was an act of self-defense and nothing else. John had threatened to shoot her dead and had gone to get the weapon. She had reached it first, and in the struggle that had followed, the pistol had gone off.

To many at the trial this was a convincing story. Remember, this John Williams had taken advantage of the girl, and had whipped her, besides.

The government, however, refused to take Fannie's explanation. By all accounts, Williams had no desire to kill Miss Echols; he only wanted to thrash her when he happened to be in an ugly mood. Nor were there signs of struggle in the death room. Persons near-by had heard no noise except a pistol shot and an exultant cry from Fannie.

"There!" the girl shouted with an air of triumph, "I've killed him!"

The victim was found in bed, in a sleeping position. A bullet had gone through his body and was lodged in the floor below—fired, apparently, by some one standing over John's reclining figure.

Murder, ruled the jury. The noose, said Isaac Parker. Fannie must hang just like the others. The Judge would not even make it a solo occasion; he sentenced her to die on July 11, 1884, with six men—five murderers and a rapist.

As a woman, Fannie Echols found it easy to get her sentence changed to life imprisonment. President Chester A. Arthur did her this favor. Fannie was then shipped off to the penitentiary at Columbus, Ohio.

Judge Parker sentenced three other women who managed to escape the gallows. They were a motley bunch—Mrs. Elsie James, an Indian; Mrs. Mollie King, a Negro; and Mrs. Mary Kettenring, a white woman.

Elsie James, a gigantic creature, did her job with a hominy pestle. She was a "well-fixed" widow who used hired men to run her farm in the Chickasaw Nation. One of her employees, William Jones, appears to have served Mrs. James in more than one capacity. Either Elsie tired of him, or else she coveted the sixty dollars he received in the mail one day in 1887. Then William Jones was seen no more.

When questioned by Deputy Marshal Heck Thomas, Elsie pleaded ignorance. At first she knew nothing, nothing at all.

How could that be? asked the officer. Had she not sold Jones' shoes?

Well, ventured Elsie, she had shot Bill Jones when he attacked her.

That did not ring true. Who would risk colliding with an Amazon like the Widow James? Maybe Elsie should think some more.

She was really innocent, she said on her third try. One of her hired hands had done the shooting, and she had helped to hush things up.

Interesting; but there had been no shooting. When officers dug up Jones' rotting corpse they found no bullet holes. Plainly, the skull had been bashed in with a blunt instrument. None other than Elsie's pestle, swung by Elsie's strong right arm.

Elsie fought the case as best she could. She even sold her farm to hire four of the best of Fort Smith's criminal lawyers. But the jury found her guilty just the same. Five days before the date set for her execution she was granted a respite. Later, President Benjamin Harrison commuted her sentence to life imprisonment and sent her off to join Fannie Echols in Columbus.[1]

Mollie King was a chambermaid in a frontier hotel. Her husband Ed was a stableboy. Finding married life just one long quarrel, Mollie and Ed agreed to live apart, but Ed dropped in to see her now and then. So, however, did other men. This led to further quarrels between the Kings, to threats and counterthreats.

Fed-up at last, Mollie lured her husband into ambush, to be set upon and shot by one of Mollie's other lovers. Ed managed to pull through that ordeal alive . . . but there was more to come.

Suddenly Mollie was all sweetness and kept asking Ed to see her; she would make it worth his while.

No, said Ed, reasonably enough—look what had happened last time.

"You want to run after some other woman," Mollie teased, "that is the reason. Why don't you come with me?"

Perhaps it was the frontier whisky, which he used very freely. Anyway, Ed decided to go along.

---

[1] After the James trial, a witness asked for Elsie's hominy pestle as a souvenir. On another occasion the son of an executed murderer requested a piece of the gallows on which his father had been hanged.

Later, neighbors found his half-stripped, bullet-riddled body. He had been shot though the back. ("He was a good nigger," said a friend, "and I didn't like to look at him.")

The case was tried in 1896, Judge Parker's last year on the bench. The prosecution tried to pin the murder both on Mollie King and on one of her friends, Barry Foreman. In the first trial the jury decided that both were guilty of murder. Then the Supreme Court disapproved of Parker's handling of the case and ordered a new trial, which came in 1897, after Parker's death. Foreman was cleared and Mollie was sent up for life.

Mary Kettenring did even better. Like Mollie King, Mary found her husband something of a nuisance and arranged for his demise. But Mrs. Kettenring did not take part in the actual killing; she only helped work out the murder plans.

To Isaac Parker she was guilty nonetheless. He saw to it that the jurors convicted her on a murder charge, and then he sentenced her to hang. Appealing the case, she won a full release three years after her first trial. The reason was clear; there was no Federal statute providing punishment for an accessory before the fact. Parker's successor, Judge John H. Rogers, made this point and he let Mary go.

In her three years in jail the Widow Kettenring won more attention than she ever had received before. Some of the notice came from Fort Smith matrons who brought her food and sympathy. The rest came from the other prisoners, nearly all of whom were men.

The Parker jail lacking a separate women's section, the girls were generally kept in a cell on the second floor.[1] In the daytime most of the male prisoners were given the run of the corridors. Though the female prisoners were kept in their cells, the men could and did stop by to talk with them.

Perhaps that was not all. Few of the girls imprisoned in Fort Smith could be called inhibited. It did not bother them to make the long trip to court in company with male prisoners and deputies, and when they spoke they voiced their thoughts in words "so obscene as to cause some of the spectators to blush." While in jail these women made a practice of shrieking scurrilous remarks at persons who passed by outside.

Now and then one of the girls caused a crisis at the jail. Such a case flared up in 1877, when Anna Jones publicly announced that Jailer Pierce had many times attacked her person.

Anna, who called herself a Civil War widow, said the affair had started soon after she was lodged in the Fort Smith jail. She claimed that Jailer Pierce unlocked her cell one day, took her to his private office, and then explained that co-operative women prisoners could expect better food than the slops fed to most of the inmates. That sounded good to Anna. She at once began to co-operate and did so "repeatedly" thereafter.

If Anna can be believed, Jailer Pierce was not the only lecher among the Federal officials in Fort Smith.

---

[1] This refers to the "new jail," built in 1889. Before that time, the male prisoners were confined in the basement of the courthouse, and the women were kept in a shack in the courthouse yard.

After her release from jail she said she had been approached time after time by nearly every officer in sight—the United States marshal, the guards, the deputy marshals. A good deal of her time in jail was spent fighting off these guardians of the law, according to her account, and as an added insult, the officers stole her money.

But Anna was a practiced liar. It seems unlikely that she ever fought off anybody. This came out in court when the charges against Jailer Pierce were aired.

"A common prostitute," said District Attorney Clayton, "one of the lowest of her kind." And a thief besides.

"Her reputation when brought here was that of a common prostitute," added United States Marshal Upham, "and she has since her discharge from jail, and is now living in Fort Smith following the usual vocation of her class, and notorious in the community as one of the most vile of common strumpets."

Yes, Anna Jones might very well have made up the whole yarn. But suppose that some of it was true —why wreck reputations on a harlot's testimony?

Jailer Pierce was cleared.

For Anna and for other female prisoners, the Parker jail did not serve as a correctional institution. Those in charge admitted as much but denied that imprisonment made the girls worse than they had been before. (Nothing could have.)

Often the officials performed such acts of kindness as they could. In the case of Anna Jones the government furnished clothes, paid freight charges on things she wanted from Muskogee and allowed the prisoner to keep her four-year-old daughter with her in jail.

This last seems nowadays like a doubtful gesture. But in Parker's day the outlook was different. The people of Fort Smith thought it best for a child to remain with the mother, whatever faults that parent might possess. The keepers of the Federal jail won praise for their willingness to board offspring as well as criminals.

Mrs. Arena Howe carried matters a bit further than Mrs. Anna Jones. Arena was brought in during the winter of 1880-81 on a charge of murder. With her came her little boy, about five years of age. And Mrs. Howe was pregnant again. She had only a few weeks to go when her case was called.

Despite her condition, Judge Parker called her case to trial. Though Prosecutor Clayton did his best to "strip the romance" from the matter, at least two of the jurors felt sorry for Arena. They held out against a guilty verdict, and Parker had to order a new trial.

The jailer's staff would have preferred acquittal, so that the expectant mother would be discharged before her baby came. But, with a hung jury, Mrs. Howe remained in jail. She had her child on schedule. What was more, the baby lived and soon accompanied mother and brother to the Detroit House of Correction. (Arena and the government had worked out a compromise plea, guilty of manslaughter.)

It was twins the next time, children of a bigamist, Nancy Brassfield, and a murderer, Albert O'Dell. Their birth was one of the features of the curious Lamb-O'Dell affair.

111

O'Dell and his friend James Lamb were itinerant farm laborers who drifted into the Chickasaw Nation in 1885. While working for two frontier tenant farmers (Ed Pollard and George Brassfield) the new-comers took a fancy to their employer's wives. Being determined young men, they soon completed their conquests, Lamb establishing himself with Pollard's wife and O'Dell with Brassfield's.

Next question: how to get rid of the husbands? The wives and their new lovers, it seems, talked over the problems together and decided on strong action. Threats first, then violence if necessary.

Disgusted or afraid, George Brassfield cleared out, leaving his farm, his wife, and his three children to Albert O'Dell. Ed Pollard proved more difficult. Perhaps he liked his wife; perhaps he hesitated to leave their child. One cannot be sure, for Ed did not live to say.

One afternoon his wife asked him to go to the near-by country store to get some kerosene and coffee. As he was tramping home he was waylaid and shot through the head by James Lamb. Albert O'Dell helped to hide the body, and the two culprits then re-joined their ladyloves, taking along the coffee which Pollard had been holding when he died.

These events took place around Christmas, 1885. O'Dell and Nancy Brassfield celebrated by getting married. Mrs. Brassfield, of course, already having a living husband, the father of her three children. But then, Mrs. Brassfield and her lover were none too bright, and strange things happened on the frontier.

James Lamb and Mrs. Pollard also sought a preacher.

It was all right, they told the clergymen; Pollard had deserted his family.

No, the minister said firmly. He was a border preacher and let a lot of things slide by. But he would not help a woman bent on bigamy.

As to the bigamy, the pastor was mistaken—the Pollard woman was a widow. But neither she nor Lamb cared to prove that point. Instead, they decided that an informal liaison would suit their needs.

When neighbors found Ed Pollard's corpse, Lamb and O'Dell had pushed along, taking their new families with them. But Captain Mershon found them and made the four arrests. When he captured Mrs. Brassfield the deputy told her that her friend Albert O'Dell had confessed everything. Nancy quickly blurted out all that she knew (and that was plenty). O'Dell, informed that his girl friend had talked, tossed in some more details.

In their wooing and assassination periods, O'Dell and Lamb had stuck together. Arrest dissolved the partnership. Hiring separate lawyers, the men attacked each other before Judge Parker. The result was a conviction for each, and a double hanging, in September, 1886.

At the end James Lamb regretted that he had turned against his partner. After all, he, not O'Dell, had fired the fatal shot. And he, not O'Dell, had acquired the dead man's wife.

"My life is enough to pay for Pollard's," Lamb said just before the date of execution, "Hang me and let O'Dell go, for he does not deserve to be hanged."

Hangman Maledon, however, strung them both up.

In this case the government chose to try the men and not the women. The latter, though, were held in jail, first as suspects, then as material witnesses. Both were expecting when they were arrested, and both gave birth just before their lovers died upon the gallows.

Around Fort Smith the general assumption was that paternity rested with Lamb and O'Dell. Date calculation shows that the problem was more complicated. Both women became pregnant before they had gotten rid of their husbands, but after they had begun to have sexual relations with their new friends.

At the time of her arrest Mrs. Pollard had only one child. This child was taken by her dead husband's brother. She managed to get out on bail before her next baby came. She was staying with her stepfather in Missouri when she gave birth to Lamb's child—or was it Pollard's?

The Brassfield woman had one child with her when she took up residence in jail, her husband having taken custody of the two others. George Brassfield, apparently, retained some affection for his erring wife, for he came to Fort Smith to be with her in the last weeks of her pregnancy. He was unable to put up bail but gave what help he could when the twin boys arrived.

Both babies died.

It was divine judgment, said sanctimonious citizens, retribution for the sins of Albert O'Dell and Nancy Brassfield . . . and yet the Pollard-Lamb child lived!

The United States Government brought no morals charges against the women in this case. That was in line with the standard practice of Judge Parker and his prosecuting attorneys. The court could easily have specialized in the punishment of fornication, adultery, incest, bigamy, and the like. But the officials in Fort Smith preferred to set sex aside and to spend their time on murder, theft, and whisky cases.

There was one exception to this general policy. When rape was involved, the Parker organization did show interest. Warrants were issued, arrests were made, and the cases were quickly brought to trial. If the evidence was weak or contradictory, the accused was given the benefit of the doubt; but where the facts were clear, the court cracked down hard. In 1893 Parker's executioner hanged five rapists in a single day.

Bigamy was taken much less seriously. Known offenders were left alone unless there was a good deal of complaint from an injured party. Even then, Judge Parker tended to be lenient. A sample sentence of 1885 called for a fine of fifty dollars and thirty days in jail.

During most terms of court there were no adultery or fornication cases. The records reveal only a handful in Parker's two decades on the bench. Of these the most celebrated concerned two of the best-educated and least offensive people ever lodged in Parker's jail —Dr. William Cooper and Mrs. Elizabeth Alexander.

The affair began in the state of Arkansas, while Mrs. Alexander was consulting Cooper in his professional capacity. The Doctor, nearing sixty, was a well-settled man, the father of eight children. And Mrs. Alexander, in her forties, seemed to be satisfied with her husband and four children.

Then, one day, Dr. Cooper recommended that Mrs. Alexander go out to the Indian country for a "rest."

Soon he too hit out for that region. He and his attractive patient were living together in a frontier community when their families located them and insisted that they be arrested.

The case was tried in February, 1890. It caused quite a stir in Fort Smith, where interested citizens took sides for or against the prisoners.

Her husband having obtained a divorce, Mrs. Alexander was tried for fornication rather than adultery and got off with a four-month sentence. Dr. Cooper was found guilty on a charge of adultery and drew a year and a half in the penitentiary at Little Rock.

Judge Parker could have been more severe. He reasoned, however, that as things went on the frontier, these two had sinned only in a minor way.

CHAPTER EIGHT

Now in Session

Juries should be led. They have a right to expect that, and if guided will render that justice that is the greatest pillar of society.

—Judge Isaac Parker

How many times have you been here before, Will Phillips?"

"Three, sir."

"For whisky, every time?"

"Yes, sir."

"Well, you seem to be one of the incorrigibles. I'll have to give you a penitentiary sentence."

Much of Isaac Parker's court work was no more exciting than that—a routine examination of a frontier bootlegger who was entering a plea of guilty. But, whatever the charge and plea, the Judge gave every case his close attention.

For one thing, he looked very carefully at all the prisoners. That was important, for the science of fingerprinting had not yet reached the Southwest frontier. Outlaws changed their names with dizzying speed, and long-time lawbreakers sometimes got by with light sentences as first offenders.

"One quart, your Honor," said Bud Impson when he was called up for smuggling whisky. This was a bid for a light fine or a thirty-day jail sentence. But Bud drew a hundred-dollar fine, plus fifteen months in the penitentiary. Judge Parker had recognized him as a repeater, recalled his Indian Territory record "down to a fine point and concluded to deprive the I. T. of his society for many months."

Parker was watching, too, when Mat Music, the rapist, made his bid for freedom. It was a blistering summer day in 1883—and summer can be very hot in Arkansas. As he glanced around, the prisoner noticed that the courtroom guards were dozing at their stations.

This was his chance to get away. Scrambling upon a table, Matt jumped to the judge's bench, then threw himself toward an open door. He had cleared the guards—but not Judge Parker. His Honor reached out, grabbed the fleeing prisoner and sent him hurtling to the floor. Matt Music did not escape.

While watching the defendants Judge Parker did not neglect the other figures in his courtroom drama. He gave a good deal of his time to the witnesses. They, after all, were the keys to all the cases that went to jury trial.

The witnesses were plain, uneducated people, and their testimony was seldom very elegant.

A crowd? "There was a heap of people there."
Acquaintances? "I knew them two."

A party? "We was on a terrible big drunk."

A quarrel? "They cussed each other for a right smart while."

How far? "I don't know any more about distance than a hog does about Sunday."

Still, these people gave fairly accurate accounts of life in the frontier country west of Arkansas. Note this picture of an evening spent in town:

> I was drinking pretty much all night . . . I was drinking and feeling pretty good—what I call drinking . . . tolerable drunk . . . I wasn't downright drunk; I was feeling pretty good though.
>
> (Breakfast "sobered me up right smart.")

Or this conversation after a gun fight—during which gun fight a bystander had said "Hell, by God, let them fight it out."

> "I am shot pretty damned bad . . . I believe I will die."
> "Don't go in there; you will bleed all over the house."

And this late evening discussion, as reported by several witnesses:

> "You damned liar, I will bust your belly."
> "Go home, God damn you; you have been raising Hell around here all night and we are tired of it."
> "You God damned cowardly son of a bitch, I am going to kill you."
> "No, I don't reckon you will."
> "You are a God damned bastardly son of a bitch and a coward and will be walking to the borders of Hell before breakfast. I will kill you tonight, or go to Hell and die fighting."

(Other parts of this exchange are unprintable.)
General conditions out in the Indian country?

Q: I suppose it was a very frequent thing up there to hear shooting?

A: Yes, sir; shooting is of very frequent occurrence.

This from the cross-examination of Henry Starr, when he was on trial for the murder of Bob Dalton's old friend Floyd Wilson:

Q: What are you carrying a gun for?

A: Most everybody carries a gun in that country. . . .

Q: That is not answering the question. . . .

A: I was carrying it simply to protect myself.

Q: Against whom?

A: Anybody. I had heard that them fellows was after me for stealing horses, and they don't generally give a fellow a trial when they catch him . . . Oh, it is just a custom, is all.

(Another outlaw put this point much more simply, saying "no damned man can make me lay down my gun.")

For another aspect of life on the frontier—the woman shortage—glance at the testimony of Mrs. Ada Bullard:

Q: What was your business there?

A: I was living there; that was my place of residence. . . .

Q: You were running a house of prostitution?

A: I suppose so. . . .

Q: A man came up and married you out of that house of prostitution?

A: Yes, sir.

Q: Did he know you were a prostitute? You would not have a man marry you without his knowing that you were a prostitute?

A: No, sir; I kept nothing secret.

Even after her retirement, Ada took pride in the fact that she had pioneered the red-light district of South McAlester, on Chippy Hill.

"I was the first person that ever lived on the Hill," she told the court, "I started out by my lone self . . . had three besides self at one time."

Soon there were competitors—Lulu May, Dolly Snow, "who sold out to Nora," and some others.

"We were always good friends," Ada explained; but standards were not the same. Ada always "tried to keep a decent place." Some of the others, she hinted darkly, sold beer at their establishments.

It might be added that Ada was not summoned into court for conducting a brothel. Parker did not bother going after madams, strumpets, and procurers; but he was interested in bawdyhouse brawls which resulted in fatalities. Ada was a defense witness in such a case. Lulu May, her chief rival, was a victim in another, being shot by an impatient customer, Marshal Tucker.

Although Tucker was a law officer, Isaac Parker had him convicted of murder. The Supreme Court found nothing wrong with the verdict, but on Parker's recommendation the White House changed the sentence to life imprisonment. No "deliberate intention to take human life."

Besides giving testimony about tours of brothels, the witnesses talked a lot about another call of nature. Such talk was not mere vulgarity; it reflected the technique of arrest in Parker's territory. After locating a fugitive the officers closed in at night and quietly surrounded the desperado's hideout. Since these shacks lacked modern plumbing, each occupant could be expected to step outside in the morning. And if the deputies were well hidden, they could delay their demand for surrender until the outlaw was least able to defend himself.

The method was many times described in the Fort Smith courtroom, often in elaborate detail.

As an example, the prosecuting attorney would ask if the man in question were standing in front of the house or at one side.

"Well," the witness would reply, "I don't suppose he would make water in front of the door."

Was the man busy when the shooting started?

He didn't have time, one witness answered, "he didn't make water. He had his tool out."

Now and again a witness or defendant would object to such a line of questioning ("nobody's business what I went out of the store for"). But these objections were rare. There was little room for prudery on the frontier.

Eager for convictions, Judge Parker often coached and encouraged government witnesses. This was notably the case in his first years on the bench.

"A reign of terror existed among them," His Honor recalled in later years. Witnesses were afraid to talk in open court. But Isaac Parker let them know that he was on their side, that he too wished to punish the wrongdoers. He could not afford much protection, but he could, and did, talk about the need for justice. And if that did not yield results he could bulldoze the witness.

Ordinarily the bullying was saved for witnesses brought in by the defense. To them Judge Parker was a terror, quick to jump on a contradiction or a lie.

Did they know what it meant to swear an oath? he asked. Would they like to have him talk about contempt of court and the penalties for perjury?

"Very strange," he grunted in one case, "that you do not know anything that is favorable to Mr. Griffith [the murdered man], and know everything against him."

"Your Harris eye was always closed," chimed in the prosecutor, "and your Griffith eye was always open."

Under the Judge's questioning, many witnesses stumbled or forgot what they had planned to say.

"If it had been an occurrence of yesterday I could probably tell it better," they would mumble, "I think so—I don't know . . . I might be wrong."

In breaking witnesses Isaac Parker co-operated closely with the United States District Attorney, the official prosecutor of the Fort Smith court. Here the Judge was fortunate; for fourteen of his twenty-one years on the bench he had as his co-worker the ablest prosecutor in the Southwest. This was William Henry Harrison Clayton[1], who took office in 1874, served until 1885, and again from 1890 to 1893.

William Clayton much resembled Isaac Parker. Both men were young when they took up duties in Fort Smith. Both were Northerners, carpetbaggers who owed office to political connections. Though neither was a careful student of the law, both had vigor, courage, and determination. Clayton, like Parker, was quick witted. When at work he gave the

---

[1] As the name suggests, Clayton was born during the Log Cabin and Hard Cider Campaign of 1840. His Pennsylvania Whig parents named him for their party's presidential candidate, Old Tippecanoe, General William Henry Harrison.

impression of being hard and mean, but like Judge Parker he was only trying to uphold the law under difficult circumstances.

Prosecutor Clayton split few legal hairs and rarely puzzled over precedents. He won cases mainly because he was (to quote Judge Parker) a "very close, shrewd, prudent examiner of witnesses."

It was Clayton's practice to anger those who appeared for the defense. An irritated witness could rarely testify effectively.

If a witness had a bad record, that was brought out in full detail. Had he done time in the penitentiary? Had he been in jail? Were there outlaws in his family? Was he a drinking man? Did he gamble? Did he frequent houses of ill fame? Did he move in low company—for example, that of the defendant?

(Although the defense objected to such questions, Judge Parker generally allowed them, as "competent to test ... reputation." But was different when the defense tried the same tactics. "Never mind that," Clayton would snap, "We do not want to go into bawdy house ... rows." And Parker, like as not, would tell the defense to stick to the case in hand.)

If talking about reputation did not bother the witness, William Clayton would try something else. As when he found that the defense witness Pete Adamson, a coal miner who ran a boardinghouse, was also a preacher for the Reorganized Church of Jesus Christ of Latter-Day Saints.

Huh, sneered the prosecutor, Pete must be a Mormon.

No, said Adamson patiently, he belonged to the Missouri, not the Utah crowd.

But Clayton kept on. The chance looked too good to miss. Polygamy was in the news, what with attempts to enforce the antipolygamy laws, and the fight over Utah's admission to the Union.

"Well," said the District Attorney, "you don't go about the men very much; it is the women you go about mostly."

Adamson flared up.

"I take that as an insult," he cried, "I did not come up here to be insulted. I would to God that you all stood as clear upon the woman business as I do."

In this exchange the Reverend Mr. Adamson kept his dignity, but he grew excited and lost some of his value as a witness for the defense.

Starting in this fashion, William Clayton often cracked a case wide open. The Pat MacGowan trial, for one. The defendant counted on a William Hunter to get him off. Instead, Hunter broke under Clayton's cross-examination and blurted out the truth. MacGowan never understood how it had happened, was still mumbling about bad witnesses when he stood upon the gallows platform.

Those on the losing side called Clayton unfair and said that Judge Parker had no right to help the prosecution. Friends of the court replied that the judge and prosecutor seldom behaved as badly as the defendant's lawyers. Colonel DuVal, who knew the situation at first hand, said that the defense of Parker's Fort Smith court was "often, very often, sustained by perjury."

When arrested, the average killer made no secret of

his record. He was more likely to boast about his deeds.

"Somebody had called me a damned son of a bitch ..." one of them said. "No damned man could live that done that."

But when coached by counsel the defendant changed his story. He was a "peaceful, law abiding citizen," he said in court; his victim was "lawless, desperate and quarrelsome."

By this time the defense attorney had prepared his case. Fees were small—ranging from nothing to about a hundred dollars[1]—and the defense could not afford to spend much time gathering evidence. So the lawyers relied on trick arguments and on the testimony of a few of the defendant's friends.

The arguments were often rather strange. Take the case of the bootlegger John Harris, who shot John Griffith after a card game. ("That damned cuss came right in there," said Griffith, "and shot me in the back when I wasn't looking.") Griffith died a few days later of blood poisoning. But, said Harris' lawyer, Griffith had used tobacco and liquor for many years. In other words, he had undermined his health before he stopped the bullet. An abstainer would have been in better shape and could have pulled through after being shot. Hence this was not a case of homicide at all.

Silly? No doubt: But the jury called it manslaughter, not murder.

[1] When a defendant had more than this, the fee ran higher. In 1885 Mrs. Lucy Watkins put up six hundred dollars for the defense of her friend Robert Wolfe who, however, was convicted.

More often the defense used lying witnesses. Cherokee Bill was recognized by several persons when he was
committing robbery and murder. Still, his attorney, J.
Warren Reed, based the defense on an alibi. Friends
swore that the murderer was miles away when the
killing took place. After his conviction Cherokee shot
and killed a guard while trying to break jail. He was
seen doing that and admitted he had done it. To his
astonishment his lawyer told the court that the victim
had been killed by a stray bullet fired by another
guard. Reed failed that time, but saved the necks of
several equally guilty clients.

Parker and Clayton were inclined to be severe when
dealing with defendants represented by attorneys as
unscrupulous as Reed. But the Judge and Prosecutor
were not always harsh. They dropped many "doubtful" cases. When they saw merit in a killer's claims,
they were willing to reduce the charge from murder to
manslaughter. In cases which did not involve murder, Parker often handed down less than the top penalty and on occasion he suspended sentence.

He did this when seventy-three-year-old Kezirah
Watson was convicted in a whisky case.

"I cannot send you to jail," said the Judge in a
pleasant tone. "You are too old a woman to send to
jail. You may go home."

Again, he was lenient with John J. Overton, the
very oldest of the thousands of defendants who appeared before the bar of justice in Fort Smith. Old
John, found guilty of fraud in a pension case, was all
of ninety-eight.

"You are too old to send to jail," was the verdict. "Go home and sin no more."

Juvenile delinquents did not fare so well. In 1886 Isaac Parker gave a jail sentence to George Washington, a boy of fourteen who had been caught stealing household furniture. The Judge lectured the boy in kindly fashion, then sent him to live with hardened criminals, all jammed together in the Fort Smith jail.

Border people saw nothing wrong in this. Bad boys should be punished, and that was that. The younger generation seemed hopeless anyway, said the *Fort Smith Elevator* when Orlando Bond, a half-wit boy, was being tried for murder (1884). Here was a case of too much education, said the editor; "he has probably devoted much of his study to the perusal of dime novels, and other yellow backed literature which is liable to unbalance the mind of any youth who sticks to it."

In discussing juvenile delinquency the frontier journalists often talked about "incorrigibles." They mentioned Alexander Allen. He was only fifteen when he took a life, in 1892. He killed a playmate, perhaps because of taunts directed at him for his color—he was Negro.

Allen's age and other mitigating factors might well have brought a manslaughter, rather than a murder, verdict. But the boy's actions kept him from getting much consideration. In jail and in court he snarled and sulked, cursed and fought, rejected kindness, and answered punishment with more defiance. Fort Smith had never seen so difficult a prisoner.

Few grieved, therefore, when Judge Parker gave

his hanging charge to the jury. The jurors called it murder and sentenced Alexander Allen to the gallows. When the Supreme Court set aside this verdict, Allen was again found guilty by a Fort Smith jury; and again, after a second Supreme Court reversal. The Supreme Court upheld the third sentence, but the White House ruled against a hanging. Allen wound up with a life sentence in the Columbus penitentiary. (Good enough, thought the Fort Smith officials, though tough on the guards at Columbus.)

In cases such as this Parker could have stayed in the background, leaving the headaches to the prosecutor, defense counsel, and jurors. Most judges did. Which only went to show, said Parker, that the bench was "not alive to its responsibilities." A judge must take a stand.

"We have had as fine juries in Fort Smith as can be found in the land," Parker explained. "They have never failed me.[1] Juries are willing to do their duty, but they must be led. They must know that the judge wants the enforcement of the law."

The juries knew that in Fort Smith. Parker left no doubt as to his attitude when he gave a jury his instructions. Spare the innocent, he said, but show no mercy toward the man of crime. Give justice to the frontier people—"teach the bad and vicious among them, that as sure as they violate the law, so will punishment overtake them."

---

[1] Actually, the Fort Smith juries were far from perfect. In hard times, hung juries increased—jurors were in no hurry to give up their three dollars a day. When irritated at such practices, Parker would swear in a jury of "best citizens." But even this did not guarantee the best results. The Judge found one of his blue-ribbon juries playing cards instead of considering a hog-theft case.

In murder cases the Judge talked for a long time, often for three hours. This gave him a chance to show the strength of the prosecution's case and to suggest that it would be fitting and proper to order the defendant hanged.

In his hanging charges Judge Parker ripped into the claims of defense counsel.

Vote acquittal, the defense had urged, there was "reasonable doubt" as to guilt.

Hold on, said the Judge. "Reasonable doubt" did not mean "any doubt and every doubt that is to sway or control the minds of rational man." No, indeed. The jury should vote conviction unless there was "real, substantial doubt of guilt, and not the mere possibility of innocence."

There was no eyewitness testimony, the defense would say; no one had seen the killing. Was it right to hang a man when there was no direct evidence of guilt?

Certainly, said Isaac Parker, circumstantial evidence was as good as any other kind. It was even mentioned in the Bible, "the evidence of things not seen." (Hebrews 11:1).

"Did you ever see your own brain?" went on the Judge. "Did you ever see your own heart?"

Of course not. And "you have never seen anybody who saw the Maker of us all?"

Well, then, why not accept in court the evidence of

things not seen? Come to think of it, the killer had eliminated the best witness—the victim. He was dead. Should that fact help the murderer?

If his client had done the deed, the defendant's lawyer said, he had killed in self-defense, as every person has a right to do.

Don't swallow this, Parker told the jury. The right of self-defense, he said, was very limited indeed. It was not enough that the defendant *thought* he had a right to kill.

Try some questions.

Was he faced with *real and present danger*—danger, not of a whipping, but of death? If he was not, he could not claim to have acted in self-defense.

Had he tried to avoid slaughter, by retreating or "using less violence than that which produces death?" If not, he could not claim to have acted in self-defense.

Were his own hands clean? Was he doing "what he had a right to do?" Or had he attacked his foe, or armed himself to kill, or goaded his opponent into attacking him? If he had done something wrong, he could not claim to have acted in self-defense.

Yes, try some questions, said the Judge. Questioning would show that very few, hardly any, Indian Territory killings were in self-defense.

If not self-defense, the crime showed "impulse," "sudden passion," said defense counsel. There was no premeditation, no malice aforethought, no willful taking of human life. It was manslaughter at most, not murder.

True, said Parker, there must be premeditation. In malice aforethought one found the "very vitals" of the "dark and bloody deed that makes murder."

But, the Judge hastened to add, there need be no long-laid plot. Murder could be planned in a moment. One could have the idea and "contemporaneously . . . and practically with the conception of it . . . execute it."

This was the nineteenth century, Parker said, an age that saw "weapons of destruction brought to such perfection that in a twinkling of an eye the heart's blood is let out . . . In a twinkling of an eye a thought to destroy human life is conceived and executed."

Premeditation, malice aforethought, willful slaying, all in the twinkling of an eye. That left little room for impulse or sudden passion.

> *It was temporary insanity, pleaded some defense lawyers. After three days of drinking cider, whisky, and Jamaica ginger Frank Carver was, by his attorney's account, in a "beastly state of intoxication . . . mentally incapacitated and deranged." No wonder he killed his mistress, the hangman's daughter, Annie Maledon.*

Foolishness, said Isaac Parker. Time after time he had told the grand jury that drinking was the curse of the frontier, that over half the crimes committed west of Arkansas were due to whisky. How, then, could one forgive a man who had overindulged? Drunk or sober, a criminal should be held responsible for his crimes.

Carver was convicted.

> *Some one else had fired the fatal shot, the defense would sometimes say. The defendant's friend, perhaps; but the defendant had stood by and had not joined in the affray. Why not acquit him and catch the real killer?*

By all means catch the killer, Parker agreed; the deputies should work on that. But meantime the jurors should not swallow all this stuff about the "innocent bystander." When two men were teamed up for evil they were equally responsible for the harm done by their wicked partnership.

The defendant had not done the shooting? But had he "aided or abetted or advised or encouraged" the actual killer? Could one excuse men willing to "stand there in reserve, ready to render . . . assistance if it becomes necessary to call them into the field of bloody action?"

No, one could not. Such men, according to the Hanging Judge, were "as guilty as though they had with their own hands fired the guilty shot."

> *In any case, the defense often said, the defendant had not been at the scene of action. His friends had sworn in court that they had seen him fifty miles away at the hour of the shooting.*

Ah, said Judge Parker, the defendant had an alibi. But the jury must remember that alibis were "easily fabricated."

Anyway, said defendant's counsel, the prosecution had been unfair. The government had brought in low-grade witnesses, and the case against the prisoner was full of holes.

Come now, the Judge would say. Prosecutor Clayton was a splendid man, a friend of all good people. The government's testimony could not be "kicked out of court by violent attacks upon it." Some prosecution witnesses did have doubtful records—what would you expect on the frontier? But "no witness is to be set aside by the mere denunciations of counsel, no matter how severe." As to the shortcomings of evidence, the jury should bear in mind that witnesses were hard to locate, and "sometimes fear deters men ... from testifying."

When he came to the defendant's statements, Parker took another line.

"You are authorized to believe those which may be against him," he told the jurors, "and to disbelieve those which would be in his favor."

Judge Parker tossed in many loaded comments. Without naming the defendants he would talk of the "deadly, hissing, burning missile," of "desperate malevolence," of a "generally depraved, wicked and malicious spirit," a "heart void of social duty and a mind fatally bent on mischief." He would speak of the "man of blood" who killed "in a diabolical and wicked way, so as to show total disregard of human life, to show a devilish purpose upon his part, to show wickedness of heart."

These words, of course, tended to prejudice the jury against the defendant. Parker took care to add that the jurors had a free right of choice. If they liked the arguments of the defense they could choose acquittal or manslaughter. But, he said with emphasis, if the prosecution was correct, "*he is guilty of murder and nothing else!*"

"You are not here to make any compromises or concessions to crime," he would say. "Uphold and vindicate the laws of this country."

Prisoners bitterly resented such instructions. After his conviction, W. H. Finch complained that His Honor "did not seem to think that I was a human being and was being tried for my life, for the jury was instructed in a most bitter, passionate and biassed manner, and void of all sympathy and mildness."

Yes, Parker's tone had been severe, and he had stretched the precedents a little. But had he done an injustice? Had he been responsible for the conviction of an innocent man?

Finch said so at the trial and for a time thereafter. He made a full confession, though, before he was hanged.

CHAPTER NINE

Parker's Hotel

What is commonly dignified by the title of the "United States jail" ... is in reality little better than a pen ... the most miserable prison, probably, in the whole country.

—Augustus H. Garland, Attorney
General of the United States, 1885

Have you seen one of our more disgusting country jails, the rat-ridden type, furnished with lousy blankets and unscoured slop jars?

If so, you can form some idea of the appearance of the United States jail in Fort Smith when Isaac Parker became a Federal judge, and for more than a dozen years thereafter.

Conditions might have been excusable if this jail had been used only as a temporary detention center, or if it had housed just a handful at a time. But the records show, that year after year, more Federal prisoners were confined in Fort Smith than in any other prison, save only the District of Columbia jail.

In those days the United States Government had no

Alcatraz, Leavenworth, or Atlanta. Long-term convicts were farmed out to state prisons—the Detroit
House of Correction and such penitentiaries as those
at Little Rock, Columbus, Joliet, Atlanta and Brook-
lyn. But the bulk of the Federal prisoners (those serving a year or less and those awaiting trial, sentence, or
execution) were confined in jails connected with the
district courts. Some of these were county jails, where
United States prisoners were boarded for about
twenty-five cents a day. Others, as in Fort Smith,
were owned, and neglected, by the national government.

Every one agreed that conditions were bad in Fort
Smith.

"A hell-hole of reeking filth," said the press,
"better adapted to the fattening of swine, than the
confinement of human beings." And none too suitable
for hogs.

"Nasty grub," reported investigating grand jurors,
"filthy mattresses on a damp and cold rock floor."

"A standing reproach," said the Attorney General's
report of 1885.

The Fort Smith jail, beneath the Parker courtroom,
consisted of two low-ceilinged basement rooms, each
twenty-nine by fifty-five feet. The floor and walls
were made of stone; and the rooms were cold in
winter, damp in summer and poorly ventilated in all
seasons.

Into these two cells were jammed from fifty to a
hundred and fifty prisoners. Segregation being im-
possible, detained witnesses and juvenile offenders were

quartered with professional desperadoes and sadistic murderers, and the sick slept with the well.

There was of course no running water. Each room (that is, each fifty prisoners) had one wash basin. The water was changed twice a day. Now and then the prisoners were allowed to take "sit-baths" in oil barrels sawed in half. The urinal tubs, one for each cell, were changed two times daily.

The patient guards tried to fight odors and disease with lime and whitewash. It was a losing battle. Year after year the jail smelled of food, sweat, urine, and tobacco juice. In the eighties the average prisoner stayed for two months and a half. That was generally long enough to impair his health. Many died in jail; others picked up ailments which shortened their lives. It is significant that the highest death rate at the Detroit House of Correction was among the prisoners shipped in from the Fort Smith jail.

Shocked by these conditions, Judge Isaac Parker called for a new deal. So did other officers of his court, and in time the Attorney General and congressmen from the Southwest took up the cry in Washington.

"Humanity demands that this state of affairs be remedied," these men maintained. A change was "absolutely necessary."

Congress, though, was slow to act. The Southwest frontier was far away, and there were many other things to do, The Indian country, which gave Parker most of his prisoners, had no representatives in Congress. And most of the congressmen from Arkansas were Democrats, out of step with the Republicans who occupied the White House during Parker's first decade in Fort Smith.

Lacking help from Washington, Parker did what he could alone. He checked bids for mattresses and blankets. He kept his eyes on food costs. (Fifty cents a day per prisoner would do the job, the Judge believed, if gouging contractors were eliminated.) Then, too, the Judge held down the jail population by dismissing minor cases and by letting many defendants out on bail.

Finally, in 1889, Fort Smith got a new United States jail. It was not a perfect structure. In fact, it was badly built. "The masonry in this place is the poorest I have ever seen," ran one report. "It is all sand and little mortar." And the building was too small. It was designed for 144 inmates; in February, 1896, there were exactly 244 prisoners confined within the walls.

Even so, the new jail was much better than the old. It was above the ground and instead of two cells it had seventy-two, arranged in three tiers. This made it possible to separate the prisoners. Those charged with capital offenses were kept on the ground floor, those taken in assault and larceny cases in the middle tier, and offenders against the liquor laws on the top floor.

At night the prisoners were put in their own cells, but in the daytime most of them were allowed to walk around and see each other. This gave them a chance to roughhouse, to swap dirty stories, and to cheat each other at craps and poker. Visitors added to the gaiety by donating smokes and gum. According to the *Fayetteville Democrat* "a jollier set of vagabonds never fattened on government rations than this motley crew of rogues."

Those who liked to look at the brighter side of things insisted that the jail was a center of educational activity. They mentioned Henry Starr, who was innocent of book learning when he took up residence in "Parker's Hotel." In the four years that followed, Starr learned to read and write and formed the habit of writing letters to the newspapers. Friends said that this indicated reform and that Henry Starr would be a decent citizen when he won his release.

Starr was pardoned in 1903 by President Theodore Roosevelt. He was killed later on while holding up a bank in Arkansas.

The Fort Smith jail was also a center of religious activity. There was no chapel in it, but there were many chances to be saved. The local clergy often visited the prisoners. So did pious laymen, people with a holy mission, or with a morbid curiosity. There were religious services each Sunday, when the inmates were exposed to much evangelism.

The preachers had their greatest success with the condemned. It was common practice for murderers to curse religion until they had been convicted, sentenced, and refused retrial. Then, as they saw that their days were few, they came round.

Some, seized with wild enthusiasm, breathed religious ecstasy as they mounted to the scaffold. Others, less demonstrative, merely accepted Christianity in the thought that it could do no harm.

Convicts not under the death sentence considered such behavior natural but, for themselves, wished no part of priests or ministers and their salvation tracts. The rejection of the tracts, of course, may have been tied up with the fact that a good share of the prisoners were barely literate or could not read at all.

There were some exceptions. In 1888, just before the shift to the new jail, one prisoner took all the religious pamphlets he could get. He seemed extremely interested—but his aim was not devotional. He assembled his tracts in Cell One, just below the courtroom, then set them on fire in an effort to burn down the jail. He almost succeeded.

Fires were not so easily started in the new jail, but there were other ways of damaging the property. Early in 1896 two Smith brothers, located on the top tier in Cell Fifty-Seven, dug their way to the roof. Lack of maintenance money kept the marshal from having the damage repaired, so the cell was left locked and vacant. But the prisoners, getting wind of what had happened, began working to connect Cell Fifty-Seven with Cell Twenty-Nine on the floor below. Operations were completed one rainy night in October, 1896. Nine men reached the roof and let themselves down to the ground with ropes made from their blankets.

They were not the first to get away. Jim Davis, alias George Meyer, and three others made it over the wall in 1888, and Joe Cross led five to temporary freedom in the winter of 1889-90.

Davis was two years at large before he met a violent death. Cross was less lucky. Returning to his rotgut-whisky peddling, he ran into United States Deputy Marshal William Ellis late one night in the frontier town of Krebs. It was too dark to aim with accuracy, but the pair exchanged shots anyway. Believing that friends of Cross were near, Deputy Ellis beat a quick retreat. He did not know that one of his bullets had struck home.

Joe Cross was found dead the next morning; "brains and blood had both flowed freely from his wounds."

"No bars can hold me" was a standard boast of the bad men brought to Fort Smith. But performance rarely matched conceit; most efforts to escape miscarried.

Loud were the boasts of Aaron Wilson and Orpheus ("Office") McGee, two frontier cutthroats tried in the early Parker period, in the days of the basement jail. Yet neither got away. Office tried four times and as often came to grief. On the last occasion Hangman Maledon and other guards pumped a good deal of lead into his shoulders, back, and arms. He survived, however, and joined his fellow braggart, Aaron Wilson, on the gallows. That was in April, 1876, when the Parker officers put on their second mass execution, a five-man show.

Some jail breaks were stopped in the planning stage. An inspection system saw to that. One routine check in 1893 yielded some iron knuckles, a three-cornered file, two knife blades, and a slingshot. At other times the searchers unearthed guns or discovered tunnels and filed bars.

Most of the trouble could be traced to visitors. Wives and sweethearts baked saws into fruitcakes or hid pistols in their petticoats. Friends worked out plans for getaways or furnished money to corrupt a guard or trusty.

Though poorly paid, the guards were very rarely tempted. An exception was E. Ferner, who guarded prisoners and also ran a peanut stand on the courthouse grounds. Late in 1883 Ferner was caught taking a file and saw to a prisoner charged with bootlegging and assault: whereupon the guard lost his job, his peanut business, and his liberty.

More frequently temptation was resisted. In 1888 a convicted killer named Gus Bogles tried to persuade a trusty to help him get outside the walls. The plan was to carry Gus out in a barrel which was used to bring in sawdust for the jail's many spittoons.

The trusty was too cautious—or maybe Bogles did not have the price. (Gus was a two-bit criminal who had helped to rob and choke to death a drunken coal miner.)

No matter. Gus would try again. Just before his time came, he snatched a pistol from a careless guard.

Again he failed. His cellmate, Emmanuel Patterson, reached over, grabbed the gun and tossed it back to the guard.[1]

Bogles was so sure he would escape that he did not even bother to get baptized. And when he stood under the noose (July 6, 1888) he did not seem to understand how it could have happened.

Gus had bad luck to the very end. The rope failed

---

[1] Like Bogles, Patterson had been convicted of murder; he had killed Deputy Marshal Willard Ayers. But Patterson had been respited, and hoped that good behavior would help him get his sentence changed to life imprisonment. It was so changed in late summer, 1888.

to break his neck, and he died a slow death of strangulation.

A much more famous case was that of Crawford Goldsby, better known as Cherokee Bill. A man of mixed ancestry, Cherokee called himself half-Indian, half-Negro, and half-white. Legend pictures him as an experienced and successful desperado. Certainly he was a villain, hard, cold, and mean; but his career in crime was brief and none too rewarding. He was taken into custody when only eighteen; and when captured he was broke.

In his few months as an outlaw Cherokee worked mostly with the Bill Cook gang. Cook, a cowboy who had turned to larceny and liquor peddling, disapproved of shooting. That enabled Bill to save his neck when he came before Judge Parker, though he did draw a stiff sentence—forty-five years in the penitentiary.[1]

Unlike Bill Cook, Cherokee Bill was fond of gunfire. While robbing a store at Lenapah he killed an innocent bystander. ("He had made a little holdup, and had got about one hundred and sixty-four dollars, and . . . he had shot a fellow.") Soon the killer's friends betrayed him for the reward—a habit among frontier bad men. Cherokee was brought to Fort Smith, tried, convicted, and sentenced to be hanged.

---

[1] Parker handed out one stiffer prison sentence—fifty-five years to the sadistic boy-bandit Eugene Stanley. In some cases Parker gave long sentences for effect, planning to ask the White House for a reduction later. This was the case with Thurman Balding of the Cook gang. Parker gave Balding thirty years, but admitted later that "it was not his intention that the prisoner should be imprisoned that length of time, his idea being that it was necessary to impose severe sentences in order to deter others." (Balding got out in ten years.)

While the case was on appeal the condemned man's friends smuggled two pistols into his cell. The guards found one of these, but Cherokee managed to hide the other. As in the case of the Smith brothers, the prisoner was aided by the poor construction of the jail. He merely dug his fingers into the mortar, pulled out a brick and shoved the gun inside.

He took it out on the night of July 26, 1895, when there were only two guards on duty at the jail.

The plan was for a general break. Cherokee Bill was to disarm the two guards while his fellow prisoners rushed the gates and went after two more weapons in the jailer's office.

One guard, Larry Keating, tried to draw. Though he was shot down, the firing gave the other guard a chance to slip away. Hearing the shots, officers off duty came rushing in and, after a good deal of shooting, forced Cherokee Bill to surrender.

By then, Larry Keating was dead. He left a widow and four children.

Of all the killings in his district, this one angered Isaac Parker most. The Judge gave his views in a public interview. He lashed out at the sentimentalists who shed tears for such border outlaws as Cherokee Bill. He denounced the government for being miserly in appropriating money for guards. He said bitter words about the Supreme Court of the United States. The court's delay in acting on appeals gave murderers a "long breathing spell," said Parker. Which, in this case, had meant death for a citizen whose life was "worth more to the community and to society at large than the lives of one hundred murderers."

Though Cherokee Bill had already been convicted of murder, Judge Parker insisted that he be indicted and tried for killing Larry Keating. The ensuing trial set speed records for Fort Smith: the jury brought in a verdict of guilty just sixteen days after Keating's death. (It was, by the way, the only conviction ever obtained in Parker's court for a murder committed in Arkansas. Parker had jurisdiction because the killing had taken place on United States property.)

With the verdict in, the Judge complimented the jurors on their speed and good judgment. He then handed down the sentence in cold, biting words.

Cherokee Bill ... you revel in the destruction of human life. The many murders you have committed, and their reckless and wanton character, show you to be a human monster ... You most wantonly and wickedly stole the life of a brave and true man ... You most wickedly slew him in your mad attempt to evade the punishment justly due for your many murders. ...

Keating ... was a minister of peace; you were and are a minister of wickedness, of disorder, of crime, of murder ... You have had a fair trial, notwithstanding the howls and shrieks to the contrary. There is no doubt of your guilt of a most wicked, foul and unprovoked murder, shocking to every good man and woman in the land.

I once before sentenced you to death for a horrible and wicked murder ... I then appealed to your conscience by reminding you of your duty to your God and to your own soul. The appeal reached not to your conscience, for you answered it by committing another most foul and dastardly murder. I shall therefore say nothing to you on that line here and now.

You will now listen to the sentence of the law, which is that you ... be hanged by the neck until you are dead.

May God whose laws you have broken ... have mercy on your soul.

After his bid for escape Cherokee Bill was kept in irons and not allowed to see the other prisoners. His lawyer won him another stay of execution but could not cheat the gallows. In time the Supreme Court upheld one of the verdicts against Goldsby. The hanging—a solo affair—took place on St. Patrick's day, 1896. Cherokee Bill was not yet twenty-one.

Most of the prisoners were sorry about Keating's death. Even Cherokee Bill.

"Larry Keating was a good man," said Cherokee, "I didn't want to kill him, indeed I didn't but I wanted my liberty. *Damn a man who won't fight for his liberty.*"

This was a fairly standard view. By and large, the prisoners liked the guards, including Hangman Maledon. Condemned men said as much when they stood on the gallows platform, and discharged prisoners also sounded praise.

Meredith Crow went all the way when he was shipped off to the penitentiary in 1886. He could not say enough in favor of the marshal, the jailer and the guards.

"I regret very much that I will be sent away from such noble great men," he said. Their "efforts to conquer weakness have succeeded." Marshal Carroll had been "extremely kind." Jailer Pryor was the "right man in the right place, for he needs no cooler to put the boys in for punishment . . . The boys think too much of him, as well as the guards, to misbehave . . . No person is allowed to speak cross to the prisoners under any circumstances whatever."

This Jailer Pryor sometimes took sick prisoners out for a stroll or to the LeGrande Hotel for a meal. (Real knives and forks; they did not have such things at the jail.) Pryor also let Mrs. William Frazier stay in the jail to care for her husband, who had lost his left arm and two fingers of his right hand in a fight with a deputy marshal.

In the same spirit most prisoners avoided giving trouble and helped the guards in one way or another. At least one prisoner gave his life in such a cause. This was John Abercrombie, alias John Robinson, alias Bronco John, a horse thief who turned nurse during an epidemic in the jail. Bronco wore himself out working night and day with the sick. Finally coming down with pneumonia, he died in jail in March, 1886.

Co-operative or not, the prisoners were hardly angels. They were rough and noisy, quarrelsome and treacherous.

"Generally rather destitute of refinement," said the *Fort Smith Elevator*, and "possessed of the devil."

The guards could not keep the criminals from shaking down new prisoners—"fresh fish"—in a kangaroo court. Nor could the officers eliminate all fights. In one of these Bud Maxfield and Eugene Stanley nearly killed a fellow prisoner. For that Jailer Pape had the offenders shackled, put in solitary, and, for a time, strung up by the arms.

When such stern measures were adopted, there were loud complaints from the prisoners and their lawyers. Cherokee Bill's attorney, for one, objected strongly to the treatment of his client. Cherokee was shackled after he killed Keating. This, said the lawyer, caused the prisoner "great suffering and pain."

More serious was the suit brought by Lewis H. Holder against Marshal Boles and his force in 1885.

Demanding twenty-five thousand dollars, Holder claimed he had been arrested without a warrant and had been hauled through cold and rain six hundred miles by Deputy Marshal Mershon. After being dumped in the Fort Smith basement jail, he had been assigned loathsome duties as a "scavenger." When illness made him inefficient he had been confined in a "cold box," a sort of coffin set on end, in which an occupant could neither sit nor recline.

In all likelihood much that Holder said was true. That, however, did not enable him to win his suit. Judge Isaac Parker was inclined to disapprove of punishment inside the Fort Smith jail, but in a dispute involving Federal officers he almost always thought it best to uphold "the law." Otherwise, he felt, the convicts would become more difficult to manage.

If there was error here it was not the gravest wrong connected with Fort Smith's frontier jail. Through the years few prisoners were punished by the guards, but many hundreds suffered because of the enforced idleness, and the exposure to filth and disease. Still greater harm was done by mixing youngsters and adults. That practice, as one writer stated at the time, amounted to opening a "school of crime and vice." And "a year's course in this school is quite sufficient for the most of them to graduate, and they go into the world to prey upon society."

CHAPTER TEN

The Gates of Hell

It is hard to . . . die upon the gallows.
—George Padgett, who did.

When Hangman Maledon gave up his job as executioner, he was asked if he feared the spirits of the sixty men whom he had sent into eternity.

"No," said old George in his solemn way, "I never hanged a man who came to have the job done over. The ghosts of men hanged at Fort Smith never hang around the old gibbet."

How about his conscience? Perhaps there had been a few good men, innocent men, among the sixty outlaws he had hanged.

Oh, no, said Maledon, he knew these frontier killers pretty well. He had come to know them in his younger days when running a sawmill out in the Indian country. He had watched the desperadoes in his years as deputy marshal and guard. The outlaws swore they were innocent even when they were standing in the shadow of the gallows. But they were lying. He had hanged a lot of liars in his day.

George Maledon was in his forties when he became a hangman. German-born, he had drifted to the Southwest as a young man. Settling down in the border city of Fort Smith, he became a policeman and deputy sheriff. He liked the work and did it well. He was not especially intelligent, but he was quick, unexcitable and attentive to details. Those qualities and his record as a veteran of the Union army won him a job at the United States jail in 1871. He stayed on, as guard and executioner, until he voluntarily retired in 1894.

A quiet, ordinary-looking little man, George Maledon was not much noticed by the press in his first years as a hangman. But as his totals mounted his fame spread. Reporters wrote him up when they described the Fort Smith court. Feature writers whipped out articles about the "Prince of Hangmen," a strange, expressionless, unfeeling creature.

Cold Maledon was, but not unfeeling. He loved his wife. He worried about his pretty daughter, Annie, who turned out badly and died a death of violence. And, like most efficient men, George Maledon took pride in his work. He was proud of having shot down several prisoners who were trying to escape, prouder still of his well-managed executions. Not a minute was wasted, and "great care taken to prevent any botch work."

In the newspapers a hanging sounded like a one-day affair.

"FOUR MORE STRETCH HEMP!" screamed the

headlines. "FIVE TRAP DOOR ANGELS SENT
TO THAT BOURNE FROM WHICH NO TRA-
VELER RETURNS!"

Such anouncements indicated that Hangman Maledon had been at work for a long time.

To begin with, he had to see to it that the gallows
was in good condition. This meant inspecting the
steps and platform, testing the hinges on the trap
door and checking on the great crossbeam. If repairs
were needed they were made; in 1886 the whole structure was replaced. The crossbeam was changed again
for the last half-dozen hangings of 1896.

(*For those who like details*: there were just twelve
steps for the condemned. The platform of the old
gallows was eight feet above the ground, the crossbeam
seven feet two inches higher. The platform measured
fourteen by fifteen feet, and the trap door, which was
hinged on both sides and opened in the middle, was
three feet across. The scaffold erected in 1886 was a
little larger all around. Like the old structure, it was
built of oak, the main timbers being twelve by twelves.
There was room for a dozen nooses, but Fort Smith
never hanged that many at a time. On two occasions
six were strung up together. There were three quin-
tuple and three quadruple executions.) [1]

Hangman Maledon also gave much attention to his
hemp. He chose ropes of the best quality, one and an
eighth inches in diameter. These he stretched and oiled
and stretched some more. This was so difficult a job

---

[1] Judge Parker planned a nine-man show for January 16, 1890; but the
White House changed two sentences to prison terms, and postponed the execu-
cution of a third man for a fortnight.

that Old George did not prepare new equipment for each hanging. He used his favorite rope for twenty-seven executions, and his second best did service nine times.

It was necessary, too, to arrange for special guards. The court used United States soldiers if there were any in the vicinity. If there were not, deputy marshals were brought in from the field.

These extras had to be instructed, to make sure that all went smoothly and that no condemned man had a chance to escape. There was a further check as to appearance. All guards were expected to dress neatly for hangings. Uniforms were introduced in 1881.

Another job was to provide new suits and coffins for the prisoners and to arrange to have unclaimed corpses carted to the cemetery. And when public hangings were abandoned (in the eighties) some one had to supervise the distribution of passes and the checking-in of the official witnesses.

While George Maledon and his fellow officers were winding up their arrangements, the condemned men were getting ready for the end. Their preparations usually stressed religion. It was natural, of course, that men should think long thoughts in their last days. And at Fort Smith such eleventh-hour reflection was encouraged by official policy. Court officers urged the prisoners to pray, advised them to talk with the preachers, allowed them to leave the jail to get baptized.

Why bother? Why not leave these murderers to their own devices?

That was easily answered, said Jailer Berry. He

"never had any trouble with malefactors after the . . . priests have begun to work with them."

As a practical person Judge Parker saw merit in that point of view. As a religious man he felt that it was his duty to make the frontier bad men think of their sins and of salvation.

"The eternal and irrevocable ruin of the soul," he said, "is a punishment infinitely more dreadful than any that can be inflicted . . . by human laws."

Save your souls for eternity, he told the men who were about to die. It could be done "no matter how many stains of blood there may be on the hands, if those hands are but uplifted in supplication to the Judge of the quick and the dead, and the heart does but speak out contrition and sorrow."

Many prisoners sneered when they listened to those words, but nearly all of them came round in time.

Thomas Thompson, who waved aside the preachers at the start, ended by putting himself at their disposal and asking that the faithful pray for his poor soul.

"Oh, Lamb of God," he said, "that taketh away the sins of the world, have mercy upon me."

Cherokee Bill, another who resisted faith, gave up poker after his conversion and tried to read the Bible. Being only semi-literate he found it rough going. He asked to be baptized and to have a prayer read as he stood waiting for the noose.

The very worst sometimes took to religion with the greatest fervor, as did Bully Joseph, W. H. Finch and Tee-o-lit-se, a villainous trio hanged in 1883. By their own admission these men had killed at least nine persons. Bully Joseph was a rapist-killer who had betrayed his partners. W. H. Finch had butchered two soldiers. Tee-o-lit-se had committed murder so that he could buy some corn liquor and go to a stomp dance. But in jail all three saw the light. They spent their last days in devotional activities, bawling hymns, and praying lustily.

"Life . . . is but a vapor," said Finch, the spokesman for the three. "It appeareth for a little while and then it vanisheth away; it is but a flash out of darkness, soon again to return to darkness. . . .

"A ray of celestial joy fills me and takes away every tear. I am now satisfied how sweet it is to die."

Calvin James and John Thornton were even more enthusiastic. James who had killed for a few jugs of whisky, gave up eating toward the end so that he would have more time for prayer. Thornton, who had outraged and slaughtered his own daughter, announced from the gallows platform that he was glad he had bungled an attempt at suicide. Survival, he said, had given him a chance to think about his sins, to repent, and pick up enough religion to take care of his "certain entrance into Heaven."[1]

While working with the clergy, the condemned men also found time to fret about appearances. Most of them wondered how they would look on execution day. They were pleased to hear that the government provided a complete change of clothing for the occasion. The new clothes came a day or so ahead of time, but few prisoners would put them on until the last

---

[1] For contrast, note the words written by Sam Williams, the Verdigris Kid, an outlaw killed by a Parker deputy in 1895: "It is hell for a man to live in the world of hell, and to be killed and go to hell, but such a fate will be for me."

minute. For, as they told the press, they wanted to look good when they were hanged.

They worried, too, about their nerve.

"I hope I will be a man," said Robert Massey, a killer who was hanged in 1883. "I hope I won't break down at the last."

Those who did collapse were much ashamed of their behavior, and hastened to explain that they were not cowards, really.

William Brown fainted on his way to the gallows.

"I have been sick for some time past," he explained when he was revived with ice water, "and am very weak."

"If I hadn't taken that poison, I would have stood it all right," said John Pointer after his collapse.

Pointer, an ax-murderer, had begged for a delay when it came time for his execution. The fifteen minutes thus obtained merely added to his anguish. He nearly fainted when he saw the scaffold, and had to be supported when he stood upon the gallows platform.

(Incidentally, he had not taken any poison.)

In their last hours, the doomed men tended to lean upon each other. A collapse, then, affected all who were about to die. After William Brown had fainted, his gallows partners became nervous and excited; and they had a hard time all round. On the other hand, defiant criminals of the James Moore type gave courage to their death-cell associates.

Many of the condemned wanted to write or dictate letters on their last day on earth. In most cases these letters were simple farewell notes, with some cheerful word about salvation.

"I have got one more day on this earth and I will die," Cherokee Bill wrote his mother, "I hope I will meet you in heaven . . . I am sorry I have caused you all this trouble, but hope you will forgive me, so good bye."

The letter was signed, appropriately, "from your son in great trouble."

Owens D. Hill, who was hanged in 1888, put more feeling into his final words.

"In God I trust in Him I die," he wrote, "O, mother, let not your heart be troubled about me, for all is well; yes, all is well . . . Jesus Christ is in me, and I am in Jesus Christ . . . I was born to die . . . 'Tis a way I never thought or dreamed of going . . . but all is well, indeed all is well,"

Hill, by the way, was known as the "merry wife killer." His wife had given a plug of chewing tobacco to her mother. Objecting to such generosity, Hill had slapped his wife. She left him; he sought her out and slashed her throat with a razor. He also clubbed his mother-in-law into insensibility.

Another killer, William Phillips, was more concerned about his body than his soul. Hanging was bad enough; but he would not stand the thought of lying out in potter's field. He therefore asked his wife to sell a cow to raise the money to ship his body home. He could then be buried properly, right next to his first wife's grave.

Phillips' last letter contained the final instructions.

"Mary," he wrote, "my slippers is to tite, i want

you to take them of to knight and lay them in the coffin, it is the last request i can make of you, don't fail to take me back to-morrow Long farewell."

Mary was certainly the loyal sort. She did as she was told, sold the cow, claimed her husband's corpse, and buried it beside her predecessor's grave. And this though William Phillips had been convicted of killing Mary's father while the old man was asleep.

An even stranger farewell note was that of Rufus Buck, the villainous leader of the infamous Buck gang. Buck decorated his message with a cross and a drawing of the Savior; but his poem reflects the urge that made him a rapist:

MY, dreAm.— 1896

i, dremP'T, i, wAs, in, HeAven,
Among, THe, AngeLs, FAir;
i'd, neAr, seen, none, so HAndsome,
THAT, TWine, in, goLden, HAir;
    THeY, Looked, so, neAT, And; sAng, so, sweeT
And, PLAY,d, THe, THe, goLden, HArp;
i, wAs, ABouT, To, Pick, An, AngeL, ouT,
And, TAke, Her, To, mY, HeArT;
    BuT, THe, momenT, i, BegAn, To, PLeA,
i,THougHT, oF, You, mY, Love,
    THere, wAs, none, i'd, seen, so, BeAuTiFuLL,
On, eArTH, or, HeAven, ABove,
gooD, By. My. Dear. Wife. anD. MoTHer
                all. so. My. sisTers

                  RUFUS, BUCK
                  Youse. Truley

I Day. of. JUly
Tu, THe, Yeore
  off
1896

```
            H
            O
            L
            Y
FATHer     Son
            g
            H
            O
            S
            T
    virTue    &    resurresur. recTion.
RememBer, me, ROCK, OF, Ages:
```

Most of the candidates for gallows justice slept well the night before their execution. Nearly all ate well the next morning. They then put on their burial clothes, talked to their religious advisers and said good-bye to their guards and fellow prisoners.

The rest went quickly. It took less than an hour, normally, from cell to coffin.

The most time-consuming job was the reading of the death warrants. In Parker's early years in Fort Smith, this was done on the gallows platform. Later, it was handled in the jailer's office. The change speeded up the show outside and seemed to put less of a strain on the prisoners.

All else followed the same pattern year after year. There was the slow walk to the scaffold, with the convicts blinking at the sun and looking for familiar faces in the crowd. Escorted up the dozen steps, the doomed men were lined up under the ropes which dangled from the great crossbeam. Then their legs and arms were tied, and the black caps were drawn over their faces. The nooses were adjusted, and the United States marshal flashed a signal to the hangman.

Many were the moods of the men about to die. Some were indifferent, some were terrified. Some were humble, some defiant. A good many failed to use the final chance to speak. Others talked till they were told that they had said enough.

Quite a few protested innocence until the very end. These men told the gallows crowd that they had been badly treated by the witnesses, by the prosecutor and the jury and especially by Judge Isaac Parker.

Take the last man hanged by Parker's order.

"I am not guilty . . ." he said from the platform. "My blood will be a stain upon those who convicted me at the Judgment Day."

But was it Parker who would suffer on the Judgment Day? This man was James Casharago, alias George Wilson. Parker rightly considered him a "moral pervert;" Casharago was a forger, a swindler and confidence man who had killed his uncle in cold blood.

Others admitted that they had killed, but blamed the Parker court for failing to conclude that the killing had been necessary.

Pat MacGowan and George Padgett, who were strung up together in 1881, made this point with vigor.

"My wife and little ones may . . . come to shame," Pat told the people who had come to see him die, "It is hard to be hanged, gentlemen, for killing such a man, who had threatened my life . . . I have served in the army for my country[1] . . . I have not been treated fairly."

---

[1] Pat was one of the three Union veterans hanged in Fort Smith. The others were William Wiley (alias William Elliott, alias Colorado Bill) and old Shep Busby.

"It is hard to ... die upon the gallows," echoed Padgett, "for the killing of a man who was a villain and should be there today. I am not guilty of murder in my heart."

Those who caught religion hardest were less inclined to complain of bad treatment.

"Oh, Lord, remember me ..." was their line, "Forgive me as I forgive."

Presumably this meant that they were "forgiving" Isaac Parker. Some said as much, adding that they were taking an appeal to a "just judge" up above. Others were content with side comments.

"I would be tempted to say a great many harsh things about my trial," said one, "but I will not do so. I forgive all my enemies, as I hope to be forgiven."

A good many, though, admitted that they deserved to be hanged, and that the Parker court had made no error. Not a few of the last speeches were confessions, complete with gory details.

The story generally had a moral, as when the degenerate John Thornton "warned all persons present to beware of strong drink, as it alone was responsible for his present condition."

Thornton, who was sixty-five, was the oldest person ever hanged on the Fort Smith gallows. Nineteen-year-old Boudinot ("Bood") Crumpton was the youngest.

Bood's story much resembled Thornton's.

"When you are about to drink a glass of whiskey," said young Crumpton, "look closely in the bottom and see if you cannot observe therein a hangman's noose.

There is where I first saw the one which now breaks my neck."

Confession or not, the murderers looked forward to a happy future.

"I bid you all a long farewell," said William Brown, "and hope to meet you in Heaven."

"As we drop out of this world together," Pat Mac-Gowan told his scaffold partners after the black caps had blotted out the sun, "let us hope we will meet in the next."

Maledon's trap doors, in other words, were passageways to Heaven. So said the condemned men, so said the priests and preachers in attendance.

Other people were not so sure; and with the passing years, the trap doors came to be known as the "Gates of Hell."

Old George Maledon would not comment on that, such things were not in his line. To him the most impressive of the gallows speeches was that of William Wiley, or Elliott, better known as Colorado Bill.

When he waited for the noose, Bill said no word about his soul. Instead, he spoke to Maledon and the other guards.

"For God's sake, boys," he pleaded, "break our necks —don't punish us."

Break the necks. That was the hangman's job. See to it that the six-foot drop was clean, that there was no struggle and no blood.

It was just that way in all but a few instances.

Robert Massey bled a little, and the blood trickled down on his coat lapel.

Both Manley brothers struggled, one drawing himself up several times before death stopped his movements. ("SICKENING!" cried the press.)

The Thornton hanging was still more revolting. This was not a Maledon affair; old George was stepping down at the last and Deputy Marshal G. S. White was in charge of the job. Perhaps the knot was not quite right. In any case, the drop almost tore off Thornton's head. Blood spurted out in streams, soaking the dead man's clothing and forming crimson pools upon the ground.

Fortunately, few saw this bloody spectacle. Orders from Washington had ended public hangings in 1881, it being felt that these affairs had taken on the aspects of a carnival. (Several thousand at each show, and lots of business for the Fort Smith saloons.)

After that, a stockade was built around the gallows, and the number of witnesses was cut down to about forty. Blown down in 1883, and burned in 1886, the stockade was rebuilt each time; and "private" executions continued to be the rule.

This was all right with the prisoners, who were noticeably calmer when the crowd was small. It was all right with Judge Parker, who felt that it was the fact (and not the sight) of hanging that discouraged prospective killers.

As for Old George Maledon, he did not care, either way. With or without a crowd to watch him, he handled the preliminaries with efficiency, then calmly pulled the lever that opened the Gates of Hell.

CHAPTER ELEVEN

Like the Withered Leaves of Autumn

The days of the Indians are drawing to a close.
—President Rutherford B. Hayes

Everywhere, at the approach of the white man, we have beheld them fade and disappear like the withered leaves of autumn before the gale.
—Judge Isaac Parker

For the white residents of the United States, the nineteenth century was one of glory and expansion. For the Indians, it was a century of degradation and defeat.

Rightly so, said most white men. In a fair fight, the better side was bound to win. That was the way of things, the way to progress and prosperity.

A few white men looked at it from another angle. As they saw it, the fight had not been fair; and there had been no need for any fight at all.

Such was the view of Isaac Parker, who was often called the "red man's friend." The Indians were splendid people, Parker said, and they were not his foes. Rather, he and they had a common enemy—the frontier outlaw, the man of crime and blood, whatever his color.

So Parker felt when he went to live on the Southwest frontier in 1875. So he felt after two decades as judge of a court having jurisdiction over Indian country.

"Twenty-one years experience . . . has taught me that they are a religiously inclined, law-abiding, authority respecting people," Parker said, just before his death, "The Indian race is not one of criminals . . . As a people they are good citizens."

The Indians were good, and yet the Indian country was a land of crime. How could that be?

It was the white man, mostly, Parker said, preying upon the Indian.

"Beyond the tide of emigration," explained the Judge, "and hanging like the froth of the billows upon its very edge is generally a host of law-defying white men—many of whom are refugees from justice —who introduce among the Indians every form of demoralization and disease with which depraved humanity in its most degrading forms is ever afflicted."

But there were bad Indians. Many of the men whom Parker hanged were members of the tribes.

Oh yes, said Parker, the Indian "has in many cases copied our vices, but failed to imitate our virtues because, as a rule, none but the refuse of our population . . . have mingled among them."

Listen to the testimony of an Indian.

"If all the whites are like the ones I know," said Little Raven, chief of the Arapahoes, "when Indian go to Heaven but few whites will trouble him there."

That was it, said Parker, the Indians had come into contact with the border bandits, the scum of the white man's frontier. The tribes had seen the vicious fugitives, the swindling traders, the cattle rustlers, the whisky peddlers, the land-grabbers and timber thieves. What could they think of the white man?

There had been friction, squabbles, and uprisings. And then the Army arrived.

That was worse, if anything, tossing the problem to such sadistic exhibitionists as the "yaller haired" Custer.

"Altogether bad," commented Parker. Under military rule, "female chastity yields to either trickery or fear; marital rights are generally disregarded, and shameless concubinage spreads its pestiferous stench through camps and lodge."

There were errors, certainly, in the civilian rule of the Interior Department, which had been in charge of Indian affairs since 1849. But when a crisis involved, additionally, the War Department, it meant "perpetual war with the Indian, and the only peace you can expect is a peace of desolation."

No, the Sheridans and the Custers could not be trusted. Handling Indians was a "peace matter," insisted Judge Parker. "Put them under . . . that civil law whose seat is the bosom of God."

What then?

Parker was not exactly sure. He knew that even good white men were a menace to the Indian. He knew that white men, good and bad, looked on the Indian as a menace and a nuisance, the more disliked because the tribes still held rich land.

Above all else, the red men wanted to be left alone. They wanted to live their own lives, to use their lands as they saw fit.

That, of course, was not to be. The outward pressure of the white man's expansion was too strong to be resisted very long. With the advancing frontier the tribes had been shoved west and south into this Indian Territory over which Parker's court had jurisdiction. And the white men were pressing hard upon the borders of this last big piece of Indian land.

What to do?

Remember first, said Parker, that we had behaved very badly in the past. Remember that our record was one of "lasting disgrace and burning shame." The Indian was poor, "poverty-stricken," "unfortunate," but he was a man in the sight of God. And he had been misused.

"The Indian has many noble qualities . . ." Parker went on. "He shrinks from no danger, and he fears no hardships . . . He is true to his country, his friends, and his home . . . If he forgives not injury, neither does he forget kindness . . . That he has been cruel and revengeful, I admit. But has he not been treated as an outlaw? . . . Has he not been driven from the land he loved?"

It was true, said Isaac Parker, that sovereign power rested with the United States and not with the Indian tribes. (The Judge would make this point with vigor in his Southern Kansas Railway decision of 1888.) But that did not justify mistreatment of the Indians.

"We must carefully and jealously guard the rights of the ward," even against ourselves, said Parker. It was time for the white man to try "honesty and integrity" in place of the old program of "broken promise and . . . broken faith."

And he, Isaac Parker, could do his bit toward that end. As a Federal judge out on the border, he could try to see that the Indians were given a square deal in court. He could work especially to rid the Indian country of the white men who were bad, and who, by their example, had made the Indians turn to evil.

But was this all worth-while? Did the good Judge think that he could save the Indian from calamity? Did His Honor think that he and his judicial robes could keep the white men from smashing in upon the tribal lands?

No, Parker was not a fool. He realized that the white men were coming. There was no disputing that. What Parker wanted was to give the Indians a breathing spell. Allow them a little while. Protect them well, teach them that there were good white men, white men on whom they could rely. Show them that there were courts which would respect their rights and punish their oppressors.

Do that, said Parker, and the "Indian may soon become convinced that his true interest is to keep pace with the progress of civilization." He could then be absorbed into the body politic, as a voting citizen; and he could join in the building of a greater and better America.

Perhaps this was asking for too much. Perhaps the white man and the Indian were too hostile to co-operate.

If so, said Parker, the Indian was doomed. There

was no middle ground between absorption and extermination.

Many Indians appeared before Judge Parker, as witnesses, defendants, and complainants.

There was Bear and White Bear, Bear Paw and Bear Tail. There was Running Deer and Deer-in-the-Water and Standing-in-the-Mud. There was Buffalo and Buffalo Face and Buffalo Chips. There was Backwater, Noisy Water, Scarce Water, Strong Water.

And Burnt Wood and Boneheart and Candy and Humming Bird and Blue Duck and Sap Duck and Tee Hee.

Runaway, Runabout, Blown Away, Saddle Blanket, One Drinker, Potatoes, Whooping Jack, Poor Boy, Mankiller, Womankiller, Galcatcher, Six Shooter, Six-killer.

The strangeness of the names seemed to be catching, for white men on the Southwest border went by such interesting aliases as Whisky Jack and Glory Bill.

These names amused Judge Parker, but did not divert him from his self-appointed task of protecting the person and the property of the red man.

In doing this, Parker counted heavily on gallows justice. String up a few outlaws, and many men would learn by the example.

At the same time the Hanging Judge cracked down on bootleggers. The government had long since learned that mixing Indians and whisky led to trouble. In consequence, Congress had passed intercourse laws designed to keep liquor out of the Indian country. But the legislation did not work out well. When he took over in Fort Smith, Parker found that the region west of Arkansas was well supplied with liquor. ("Very mean whiskey," much of it, "pisin," "regular rotgut," or "Choctaw beer," a vile drink made of barley, hops, fishberries, and tobacco.)

The results were pretty bad.

"Whiskey flows very freely about Atoka," wrote Deputy Marshal Dave Layman, who was later killed by bootleggers. "Cases of drunken lawlessness and dissipation have been common there for some time past. Shooting up houses, running horses at breakneck speed through the streets, whooping, yelling, and creating an especial pandemonium in the town, about once a week, is the sport of a few of the blades, when whiskey runs free."

Worse than that; the illicit-liquor traffic was linked with other types of crime. The small-time whisky peddler generally had a criminal side line.[1] Bigger operators combined bootlegging with rustling or land-grabbing.

Altogether, liquor was "a fruitful source of evil, disorder, and crime. . . ." said Indian Agent D. M. Wisdom, "a many headed demon."

"Expect no mercy," Parker told the whisky crowd. He was out to wreck them and clean up the Indian Territory. And he was especially interested in the big bootleggers, like Julius Henshaw and Francesco Rocco. (Rocco had cleaned up plenty and was getting ready to return to his native Italy when Parker caught him

---

[1] When a deputy marshal arrested George Jackson, he found several bottles of red whisky in Jackson's carpetbag; also cards, gambling chips and loaded dice. "George was prepared to meet the boys on any ground," said one reporter. "If he could not sell the liquor, he could give it to them, and win their small change after getting them drunk."

and gave him a five-year term in the Detroit House of Correction.)

To stamp out drinking, Parker even went beyond the letter of the law. The intercourse statutes banned spirituous liquors and wine, but did not mention lager beer. Anheuser-Busch and others therefore chose to test the laws, to see if they had the legal right to ship beer into the country of the Indians. They won their case in the Federal court in Paris, Texas; but they were beaten in Fort Smith.

No beer, ruled Judge Parker. The intercourse laws were intended as prohibition measures. The term "spirituous liquors or wine" meant intoxicants; and beer was an intoxicant. Besides, Tacitus had said that beer was like wine.

Foolishness, said the Supreme Court (*Sarlls v. U. S.*, 1894). Tacitus and Parker were dead wrong. All the best dictionaries agreed:

(1) "Spirituous liquors" meant distilled liquors. Rum, brandy and whisky were distilled. Beer was not.

(2) "Wine" was made by the fermentation of the grape. Grapes were not used in making beer.

The sale of beer to Indians was an "acknowledged evil," said the learned judges; but it was not illegal. Isaac Parker had succumbed to the "temptation . . . to stretch the law."

In this instance Congress stepped in and changed the law, adding beer to the list of liquids barred from the Indian Territory. But, time after time, Judge Parker was unable to help the Indians because of some defect in the law.

Take extradition. The law said that fugitives could be shipped from one state or territory to another to stand trial. But, as Parker ruled in *Ex parte Morgan* (1883), the Indian country was neither state nor territory. In consequence, the tribes had no way of getting hold of an Indian criminal who had fled to Arkansas or Texas. Nor could the Indians get rid of men wanted in Kansas or Massachusetts by turning them over to those states for trial.

Too bad, said Parker, it was a shocking situation, but "the courts do not make the law."

It was the same with the timber thieves. Some of these were petty criminals. Others (notably the railroads) worked on a large scale, stripping the tribal lands of a valuable resource.

There was a Federal law covering this type of plunder. It applied, however, only to "lands of the United States." Now, Indian lands were not "lands of the United States." Hence Federal judges could not punish timber thieves operating in the Indian country. Nor could the tribal courts take jurisdiction, unless the offender happened to be an Indian.

Parker thought this situation very bad, and denounced the timber thieves on more than one occasion.

"A class of men . . ." he said in *U.S. v. Reese* (1879) "who revel in the idea that they have an inherent, natural right to steal from the Indians."

"There should be a law," the Judge continued. "If the law-making power will give us a law, we will lay its mailed hand upon its violaters in such a way that the timber in the Indian territory will be protected from the rapacity of those who are now stealing it."

There should be a law; but there was none until nine years later.

The Indians were also bothered by the cattlemen, who drove their herds through the Indian country and used tribal pasture land without permission. Again, however, there was no satisfactory legal remedy. When the Cherokees tried to enforce a grazing tax by seizing cattle, Parker ruled that the seizure was illegal (1876).

"The mere fact of a man being in the Indian country without a permit is no excuse for seizing his property," said the Judge. "Neither the Indian Sheriff nor any other officers of the Indian country can seize him nor remove him or his property."

Could anything be done?

Well, the Cherokees could appeal to the Federal government to expel the intruders under the intercourse laws. But, as the Indians knew and as Parker knew, that was no permanent solution. The white men would keep on coming.

Twelve years later Parker ruled that the Creeks had no authority to fine the Saginaw Cattle Company, which had been grazing stock on Indian lands. It was a pity; but the Creeks were not allowed to assess fines against white men.

In these cattle cases Parker disappointed the Indians.[1] But the Judge did please the tribes when he took on the notorious Oklahoma Boomer, David L. Payne.

---

[1] The Indians had other complaints about the court. They objected to travelling the great distances to Fort Smith. They claimed that some Parker deputies cared more for fees than justice; and they felt that many Parker jurors were anti-Indian. ("They seam afraid," said one observer, "Fort Smith is such a terror to all Indians from the lowest to the Highest.")

Payne was a crusading white frontiersman obsessed with the idea of smashing the Indian monopoly of the lands west of Arkansas. He was backed by other land-hungry farmers; also by railroad interests. Congress had granted several railroad companies right of way through the Indian country and had voted these companies land grants, where, when, and if Indian titles were extinguished. The railroads, therefore, were as anxious as was Payne to cut into the tribal lands.

Payne and Parker clashed over the ceded or unassigned Oklahoma region. Though earmarked for the Indians, this area was not assigned to any tribe from the late sixties to the eighties. Claiming that white men could homestead or pre-empt the land, Payne's Boomers moved in. Tossed out by government officials, they tried again; whereupon the United States Army hauled Payne to Fort Smith for trial as an intruder under the intercourse laws.

No more important case had ever come to Parker. The Indians appropriated money to assist the prosecution. After all, they said, if the court upheld the Boomers, it would "legalize the overwhelming of our whole territory." Payne was also opposed by white cattlemen who leased the ceded lands. And by a few white men who felt, with the *Border Minstrel* of Guthrie, Kentucky, that the Boomers were "committing land piracy and highway robbery on the poor Indians."

Lined up on the other side were the railroad companies and white frontiersmen generally. These people were anti-Indian on principle. Besides that, Boomer Payne claimed that he was the victim of the "rascality" of "certain high officials," behind whom were the "powerful moneyed influence of the cattle kings who are using the country as grazing fields."

Payne had many sympathizers in Fort Smith.

"BAYONET RULE!" screamed the *Elevator* when the Boomer was brought in under military guard. This Payne had "the stuff pioneers are made of," he was "such a man as Daniel Boone . . . would have given a warm welcome."

"Time has been . . . when the government encouraged and applauded the western pioneer," the editor continued. But now "citizens engaged in peaceful and lawful pursuits" were arrested and persecuted . . . through the malice or misguided zeal of U. S. officers in the Indian country."

Back in his Missouri days Isaac Parker might have listened to that type of appeal. He had then believed in territorial organization for the Indian country, and the admission of white men into the territory. But as a frontier justice, he came to feel his "sense of duty to do equal and exact justice to the Indians, and to give them that full measure of justice which by law and good conscience belongs to them."

That of course meant cracking down on Boomer Payne. Parker did so in a decision of 1881. Citing many precedents, the Judge ruled that the lands in question, though unassigned, were clearly a part of the Indian country. Pledged to keep white men out of the Indian country, the United States Government had adopted the intercourse laws. These provided for the expulsion of white persons who tried to live there without permits. Second offenders could be fined a thousand dollars.

That was the law, said Parker, and "it must not be expected or asked that . . . the courts will break or even bend the timbers of the law."

In other words, the Boomers must stay out; and David L. Payne was fined one thousand dollars.

That was the limit of the statute. Had there been provision for a prison sentence, Parker would probably have added that; for the Judge agreed with Attorney General Brewster, who wrote the next year that Payne was "an old and notorious offender, and deserves severer punishment than can be meted out to him in the present state of the law."

Even so, the Parker ruling helped the Indians. The tribes celebrated the decision as an important victory, while the Boomers viewed it as a real setback.

In 1885 Parker again backed the Indian against the Payne crowd. Connell Rogers, an Indian official, was being charged with arson because he had set fire to a shanty built by white intruders just south of the Kansas border.

The case gave Parker a double opportunity. For one thing, he could protect and uphold an Indian official. This pleased the Judge, who had long co-operated with tribal representatives and with the Indian police, who acted under the Indian Agents. In addition, Parker was able in his Connell Rogers ruling to establish Cherokee ownership of a vast disputed area—the so-called Cherokee Outlet.

This was important; but Parker could not stop white migration into the Indian country. By the late eighties white men swarmed all over the region west of Arkansas, outnumbered the Indians on Indian soil.

As their numbers grew, the new settlers demanded —and obtained—consideration from the government in Washington. The unassigned lands which Payne had coveted were opened to white settlement in 1889, and were the basis for the white-dominated Territory of Oklahoma, organized the next year. The Indian Territory, north and east of Oklahoma, remained under tribal control, but there too the white residents made demands. Specifically, they wanted to end Parker's power, to have courts of their own out in the territory.

Neither Parker nor the Indians approved of this proposal.

"A fearful blunder," said Judge Parker. "A grievous mistake." Federal courts out in the Indian country would use white jurors of that region; and no Indian would get a break.

"Judge Parker is good enough for any law-abiding country," agreed two Indian spokesmen. If the Judge lost his power, it would pass to the "land grabbers, townsite boomers and vigilanters . . . who . . . are striving daily to rob the Indians of what they have left of what is justly theirs."

But there was no resisting the new pressure. In 1889 Congress decided that Federal courts should be established in the Indian country. Powers were limited at first, but a law of 1895 gave full authority to Indian Territory courts and (as of September 1, 1896) ended Parker's jurisdiction over country west of Arkansas.

The Indian, however, did not forget the Hanging Judge.

It was the Five Civilized Tribes that knew him best —the Cherokees, Creeks, Choctaws, Chickasaws and Seminoles. After 1883, Parker's jurisdiction west of Arkansas had been largely confined to lands owned by these tribes.

His Honor missed no chance to praise these Indians; he was "their defender on all occasions."

"They are today a civilized, Christian people," he said. They had laws "as intelligent and as accurate in language and in intent as any laws" passed by Congress.

Yes, Parker continued, they were splendid people and had set up efficient governments. The Judge did not agree with those white men who favored breaking up the tribal organizations as soon as possible.

The Five Civilized Tribes, in turn, gave praise to Isaac Parker.

The Indian people . . . have lost one of their staunchest friends [said their representatives when Parker died] and one of the ablest and most consistent defenders of their rights under the treaties with the United States. The good people of the Territory knew him to be an upright judge, a lawyer of towering ability, a citizen of the very highest standards, a gentleman of the most refined character, a friend of unswerving fidelity and an example to society.

CHAPTER TWELVE

Murder on Appeal

The appellate court exists mainly to stab the trial judge in the back and enable the criminal to go free.

—Issac Parker's opinion of the
Supreme Court of the United States

For a decade and a half (from 1875 to 1889) Judge Parker ran his court as he pleased. Then Congress changed the rules—gave the Supreme Court the right to review the important criminal cases.

Until that time, Parker's authority had been almost complete. Prisoners whom he sentenced to the gallows had only two moves left:

(1) they could ask the Judge for a retrial; or

(2) they could beg the President of the United States to change their sentences.

Either way, Parker had the whip hand. He could allow or deny motions for new trials; and his rulings were final. Then, too, he could and did influence White House action in pardon cases. ("The judge is

179

so little given to recommending pardons," said President Grover Cleveland, "that . . . I think I am safe in following his judgment.")

After 1889, the situation changed. Convicted murderers could appeal to the Supreme Court, where Parker had no influence at all. And, more often than not, that high tribunal decided against the Fort Smith court, releasing the prisoners or ordering a new trial.

Let us be specific. Forty-six of the men and women whom Parker sentenced to the gallows appealed their cases. The Supreme Court ruled that thirty had not had fair trials. Of these thirty, sixteen were then discharged, or won acquittal on second trial. The rest wound up in the penitentiary, most of them having been found guilty of manslaughter.[1]

The reversals did not altogether stop the wheels of Parker's scaffold justice. After all, the Supreme Court did accept sixteen of Fort Smith's death sentences. That left some business for the gallows—so much, in fact, that there were ten hangings in Parker's last year, 1896. But many worthless necks were saved. Henry Starr, for instance, and Eugene Stanley and Buzz Luckey, three of the worst bandits who ever infested the Southwest.

---

[1] Seven of these fourteen were convicted of manslaughter at the second trial; the other seven were found guilty of murder. One of the latter, Mollie King, was sent up for life, under a statute of 1897, which allowed juries to substitute imprisonment for capital punishment. The half-dozen others once more appealed to the Supreme Court, which again reversed Fort Smith. One of the prisoners involved was sent to an insane asylum, while three drew prison terms. Two, John Brown and Alexander Allen, were for a third time convicted of murder and sentenced to be hanged. Brown won a third reversal from the Supreme Court and settled for a one-year sentence. Allen's conviction was affirmed by the Supreme Court justices, but his sentence was changed to life imprisonment by the President.

Why these reversals? How was it that the learned justices let bad men get away?

The Supreme Court's answer can be stated in two words: *reversible error.* Sometimes Parker had gone beyond his jurisdiction, trying cases which belonged in the tribal courts. Sometimes the Fort Smith officers had failed to follow proper trial procedure. And, time after time, Judge Parker had deprived defendants of their rights by misstating the law in giving his instructions to the jurors.

There was something to this. For a decade and a half the Fort Smith court had been virtually unsupervised. In that period the court officials had slipped into bad habits. Forms had been filled out carelessly, and in his jury charges, Parker had sometimes done violence to legal principles.

As in the interpretation of flight.

When a suspect runs away, his flight is a fact to be considered at his trial, "a proper fact to be taken into consideration as evidence of guilt." But of itself, without supporting evidence, flight does not prove guilt.

Parker knew that very well, and often stated it correctly. Now and then, however, he could not resist quoting scripture against objectionable defendants.

"The wicked flee when no man pursueth," was one of his favorites, "but the righteous are as bold as a lion." (Proverbs 28:1.)

Parker used this quotation in charging juries sitting in judgment on Sam Hickory, Ed Alberty and Henry Starr. Each time the Supreme Court sent the case back for retrial.

"Fatally defective," said the justices. Good theology, perhaps, but bad law.

It was the same when Parker used the story of Cain and Abel to show that the testimony of a killer was bound to be false.

"Plainly erroneous," ruled the Supreme Court. "Men may testify truthfully although their lives hang in the balance."

Now and then, the high tribunal understandably objected to the tone of Parker's instructions.

"The charge . . . crosses the line which separates the impartial exercise of the judicial function from the region of partisanship. . . ." said Justice Edward D. White in passing on Hickory's second appeal. "Reason is disturbed, passions excited, and prejudices are necessarily called into play."

In this instance one can go along with White; but it does not follow that the Supreme Court was always right in ruling against Parker.

It was not. Whether we judge by law or common sense, the learned justices were often wrong. They stressed the form and not the substance of the law, they based key decisions on the most doubtful technicalities.

There are many pious folk who feel that laymen should not criticize so exalted an outfit as the Supreme Court of the United States. Very well; let the court speak for itself.

In 1896 that high tribunal reversed Judge Parker in a manslaughter case (*Crain v. U. S.*) The reversal was based on a minor defect in the court record, the "merest technicality." The defendant had suffered no injury by reason of this technicality, and his attorney had taken no exception on this point. Nevertheless, the Supreme Court took up the matter and ordered a retrial.

"To reverse the judgment . . ." said Justice R. W. Peckham in a dissenting opinion, "is . . . a sacrifice of justice to the merest and most formal kind of objection, founded upon an unjustifiable presumption of error and entirely at war with the facts."

On that occasion Peckham spoke for the minority; but in the long run his view would prevail. Eighteen years later the whole court would declare that there had been scant reason for the reversal of Judge Parker in the Crain case.

It was Justice William R. Day who announced the new line, in *Garland v. State of Washington*, 1914.

The court of 1896, said Day, had leaned too heavily upon the English common law, and had overstressed a "wholly unimportant formality." "Under present systems of law," there was no need and no excuse for "such strict adherence to the mere formalities of trial." The "better opinion" was in the dissent; and it was clear that the sentence pronounced by Parker should have been upheld.

In other cases, too, the present-day reader will feel that the Supreme Court too often split hairs in considering cases appealed from Fort Smith. And, as in the Crain case, one frequently feels that the "better opinion" was that of the minority.

When it saved John Brown's neck for the third time, the Supreme Court said that Parker had committed reversible error in stating that reputation could not be founded on the "judgment of bad people, the criminal element, the man of crime."

Case reversed, said the majority, "the instruction given was too narrow and restrictive."

Come, come, said Justice David J. Brewer in his dissent. Parker's comment was "just and sound," for reputation was not "made up by the flippant talk of a few outlaws."

Anyway, said Brewer, there was a larger issue:

After three juries, thirty-six jurors, have agreed in finding a defendant guilty . . . and such finding has each time been approved by the trial judge, the judgment based upon the last verdict ought not to be disturbed unless it is manifest that the verdict is against the truth of the case, or that the court grossly and prejudicially erred.

This Justice Brewer stood up for Parker on other occasions, too, scolding his colleagues for specializing in the minor technicality, the "refinement of criticism which offends common sense."

"Ought the deliberate judgment of twelve men as to the defendant's guilt, approved as it was by the judge who presided . . ." he asked in 1893 (*Graves v. U. S.*) "be set aside for an error, if error it be, so frivolous as that?"

Brewer also objected to the Supreme Court's assumption that Fort Smith habitually did things wrong.

"When," he asked in the Allen case, "did it become a rule of law that a court of error should presume that the jury in a trial court were ignorant?"

"We are not dealing with the mock scenes and shows of the stage . . ." he added when his colleagues ordered a new trial for John Hicks. "Great injustice is being done to the government and wrong to the public."

Justice Brewer had common sense on his side—and one excellent legal argument. When considering criminal appeals, the Supreme Court was by its own rules supposed to confine itself to the issues raised by the prisoner's lawyer in his bill of exceptions. These exceptions had to be specific, and the prisoner's lawyer was not allowed to appeal on points which he had not raised at the trial.

Despite such rules, the Supreme Court often decided Parker cases on points not raised by the prisoners' lawyers. Instead of insisting that the exceptions be specific, the justices allowed lawyers to take general exceptions, as to the whole of a forty-page charge. Time after time, therefore, Parker was reversed when "no sufficient exception was taken."[1] In other words, the Supreme Court was more likely to use technical points against Judge Parker than in his favor.

Why so?

Partly, no doubt, because the Fort Smith judge indulged in open criticism of the Supreme Court.

Parker was much worried over the reversals.

"For twenty long, laborious years . . ." he said, "I have sought to protect innocent human life . . . to enforce and uphold the law of the United States against the man of crime." And now, in the twilight of his

---

[1] The court would say, as in *Allison v. U.S.* (1895), "exception was taken, not with much precision, but, we are disposed to hold, sufficiently to save the point." Similarly, in the Dennis Davis insanity case that same year, the justices ruled against Judge Parker, although they admitted that his position was "not without support by adjudications in England and in this country."

life, he found his work threatened by the rulings of a higher court. It was like a stab in the back.

Murders are . . . on the increase . . . [Parker told the St. Louis press in July, 1895.] I attribute the increase to the . . . Supreme Court . . . The murderer has a long breathing spell before his case comes before the Supreme Court; then . . . the conviction may be quashed . . . upon the flimsiest technicalities. The Supreme Court never touches the merits of the case. As far as I can see, the court must be opposed to capital punishment, and, therefore, tries to reason the effect of the law away.

Seven months later, the Judge again spoke out against the Supreme Court's "mania for reversing murder cases." These "numerous and unwarranted reversals," he said in a public letter, tended to "embolden the man of blood, thus increasing murder."

"The people should demand of the courts that they discountenance intrigue and hair-splitting distinctions in favor of the criminal at the expense of life," he told the grand jury that same month. "This is the glaring evil that is sapping the life and power out of the nation."

Friends of the Supreme Court hastened to defend that body and to accuse Parker of bad taste. How could a judge and lawyer talk that way!

"Honest and true criticism is not abuse," Parker publicly replied. He had the "greatest respect" for the Supreme Court, but found it necessary to "condemn its most grievous errors and blunders in cases where there is no manner of excuse for their existence."

"No such line of crude, inconsistent, frivolous and absurd grounds for the reversals of murder cases can be found as having emanated from the appellate court of any civilized country," he continued. "They show want of knowledge of either the facts or the law of the cases. Many of them show the venom of the judges against the trial judge, apparently because they have to decide the cases. They seem to think he is the author of the crimes."

Speaking from his deathbed, in September, 1896, Judge Parker still held his ground.

No, he would not "dream of destroying" the right of appeal; but he thought the government should set up a special appellate court, the judges to be learned in the criminal law. Supreme Court justices, he pointed out, were "men from the civil walks, and it is not surprising that they are liable to err in criminal cases."

"I would that the law would provide against the reversal of cases unless innocence was manifest . . ." he added. "I would have brushed aside all technicalities that do not affect the guilt or innocence of the accused."

While denouncing the Supreme Court, Parker also sounded off against the Attorney General, the Solicitor General and their assistants. These Justice Department officers were supposed to speak for the Fort Smith court when cases went up on appeal. But, said Parker, they blundered badly and let the opposition run off with the show.

In one way this was understandable. The average Attorney General of the nineties knew little about criminal law and less about the frontier. His aides were in the same position, hence could not compete with the experienced criminal lawyers on the other side.

Take the first reversal suffered by the Parker court —*Alexander v. U. S.*, 1891. Augustus H. Garland was counsel for Alexander, while the Solicitor General, William Howard Taft, appeared for the United States.

It was not an even match. Taft was an able lawyer who would in time become President of the United States and Chief Justice of the Supreme Court. But he was young in 1891, and his training and background had taught him little about frontier murder cases. Garland, on the other hand, was well equipped to help his client. He was an old hand at Federal practice, and had been Attorney General under Cleveland. More important, he knew Fort Smith well, for he was an old-time Arkansas attorney, and was rated one of the best lawyer-politicians of the Southwest.

Parker let that one pass; after all, Taft had done his best. But some Justice Department officers did not even try. Had they chosen to exert themselves, they might have prevented several of the reversals of 1895 and 1896. But they were not much interested; and on six occasions they gave up without a struggle, confessing error and agreeing with the opposition that there should be a reversal.

This was more than Isaac Parker could endure. It was bad enough to be reversed; it was worse to lose cases by default. In February, 1896, therefore, His Honor stated his opinion in an open letter to Attorney General Judson Harmon.

He was surprised, he said, greatly surprised at the "unprecedented and unwarranted," and "extraordinary and unwise" decision of the Justice Department to confess error in the "most diabolical and wicked murder cases."

"Liberty and . . . life," he warned, "are precarious unless those in authority have sense and spirit enough to defend them under the law."

As judge in Fort Smith, he had done his bit. The "blood of the innocent murdered victims" was not on his head. Could the Attorney General say the same? Or had he encouraged the bad men of the border, the "criminal horde" that Parker had fought for so long?

Harmon replied with vigor, through Assistant Attorney General Edward B. Whitney.

Parker meant well, sneered Whitney; but he was ignorant or careless. The Justice Department had tried to instruct him, but the Judge had continued to pack his charges with "very gross errors." These errors, Whitney added, were "the more to be deplored because in most cases the prisoners are probably guilty and would have been convicted if the court had submitted the case with the very barest statement of law of murder and without any denunciation or attempt to usurp the jury's functions."

"The judge . . . is, on account of his great desire to secure convictions, the best friend of the criminals," said Whitney in closing, "for he insures them reversals, and thus gives them chances of escape which the most adroit criminal lawyers could not possibly accomplish."

"A bitter personal screed," snapped Parker when he saw Whitney's effort, "filled with the grossest misrepresentations, with manifest prevarications, and with lame attempts at the suppression of facts. It is not original, for I have heard it croaked by every foul bird of evil, hissed from every wicked serpent of crime, and yelled by every Fustilarian for all these twenty years."

Warming up, the Judge termed Whitney's arguments "outrageous," "wholly untenable," "radically wrong," "feeble and childish," "insulting," "filled with gall, with bitterness and poison." Whitney himself was "wholly incompetent," a "legal imbecile," "lacking in judgment or decency," "a man who has never tried a murder case in a trial court in his life" and who knew "absolutely nothing of criminal law, any more than he does of the hieroglyphics on the Pyramids." Such "mental pygmies," by reason of their "ignorance" and "sublime impudence," stood "on the side of the man of crime, the man of blood."

Savage though it was, Parker's reply to Whitney was not mere denunciation. It was also a spirited defense of the Judge's position. Citing authorities, he argued that his instructions to the jury were legally correct.

In the end, however, Parker rested his case on moral rather than on legal grounds. Legal niceties aside, he and his court deserved better treatment than they had received from the Justice Department and the Supreme Court. After all, he said, he had "for four lustrums been aiding in the great battle between the law's supremacy and . . . human life and human rights on the one hand, and the bloody, wicked, unrelenting man of crime on the other." That was the important thing.

Whitney, of course, could not agree. But others did. Parker had a job to do, a tough and nasty job; he had to fight the "worst bands of desperadoes, murderers and outlaws to be found in any civilized land." Where possible, he observed all the rules of law; but he had no time to deal in technicalities.

Philander C. Knox, Theodore Roosevelt's Attorney General, said as much in later years when he discussed the Parker trials.

"Many of them were conducted without the regard to the rights of defendants which prevails in more settled and law abiding communities," concluded Knox, "and ... many convictions were obtained which could not have been obtained elsewhere." But "this condition was perhaps the almost necessary result of the state of affairs which existed in the Indian Territory in the days when the Territory was infested with outlaws and desperadoes, and murder and robbery were everyday occurrences."

CHAPTER THIRTEEN

Gone are the Gallows, the Judge is Dead

We have been enabled to arrest the flood tide of crime.
—Judge Issac Parker

James Casharago, who was hanged on July 30, 1896, was the last man to die on the Fort Smith gallows.

One month later, on September 1, 1896, Parker's court lost its criminal jurisdiction over the country west of Arkansas.

"Oyez, oyez," droned Court Crier Hammersley, who had been with Parker for a decade and a half. "The honorable district and circuit courts for the western district of Arkansas, having criminal jurisdiction of the Indian Territory, are now adjourned. God bless the United States and these honorable courts!"

Judge Isaac Parker was not on hand to hear those words; he was lying home in bed, sick unto death.

It was Bright's disease, said the doctors, dropsy, heart trouble, and complications. Not to mention overwork for twenty years.

Well, said the patient, it had been important work.

He would not have changed his life if he had it to live again.

Come to think of it, he had passed up one good opportunity. In 1889 President Benjamin Harrison had offered him a much easier job, as judge of the Eastern District of Arkansas. But Parker had refused.

"I regard the court here," he had said, "as one of more importance to the country."

He had worked hard in this border city of Fort Smith. He realized that as he looked back over his two decades as Federal judge.

"The great battle," he believed, had been worthwhile. To be sure, there had been disappointments. Congress had never provided sufficient funds, and the statutes had been woefully defective. Some of Parker's work had been undone by the Attorney General and the Supreme Court. And the Judge felt that Congress had been overhasty about giving full authority to courts out in the Indian Territory.

But much had been accomplished, even so. The years from 1875 to 1896 had been years of trouble for the Indian country, and years of growth. The population had jumped from sixty to three hundred thousand; and as the numbers grew so did the conflicts and the crimes. No man could have handled all the problems which arose. But in those times of turmoil one could battle for the right. That Parker did; and as he reviewed his career, he knew he had fought well.

"This court has done more than any other court anywhere to uphold the laws of the land . . ." he said not long before he died. "It has taught a great object lesson to the people of all the West, and that is that they must rely upon the strong judicial arm of the Government when that arm is upheld by a court and jury and officers whose mission they understand to be to sustain the innocent by punishing the guilty."

Judge Isaac Charles Parker died on November 17, 1896, and was buried in Fort Smith, near the court which he served, near the people he had loved.

Many mourned his passing, and spoke of him as the greatest frontier judge America had ever known. But there was no tribute more touching than that of that Indian maiden Sadie Dove, who gathered some wild flowers and placed them on Parker's grave.

A Note on Sources

A great cyclone wrecked the Parker home soon after the Judge's death. This storm seems to have destroyed the family's personal papers. Fortunately, however, Parker's story can be traced from other records.

His court is still in session, although its jurisdiction is now confined to Arkansas. But the manuscript court records for the Parker period have been preserved. I have used them extensively.

These Fort Smith manuscripts are supplemented by the unpublished records of the Justice Department in the National Archives, Washington, D.C. The Grant Foreman MSS., Oklahoma Historical Society, contain Parker material, in tribal correspondence and manuscript reminiscences. (Indian-Pioneer History).

No less important are the contemporary newspapers. The history of Parker's court is well told in the news items of the *Fort Smith Elevator*, the *New Era* and the *Times*. I have also used the *Arkansas Gazette*, a Little Rock paper with fair Fort Smith coverage. The St. Louis press, especially the *Globe-Democrat* and *Re-*

public, carried a good deal about Judge Parker, who usually released his public statements through St. Louis. And I found a surprising number of Fort Smith items in two New York papers, the *Herald* and the *Tribune*. I have also used the *Gazette* and *Herald* from Parker's home town, St. Joseph, Missouri; and three Indian Territory papers: the *Cherokee Advocate* (Tahlequah), *Indian Journal* (Muskogee, Eufaula), *Indian Chieftain* (Vinita).

Quite a number of Parker's decisions are printed in the *Federal Reporter*. Supreme Court rulings in cases appealed from Fort Smith are found, among other places, in the *Supreme Court Reports*. I have printed a couple of Parker items in the *Arkansas Historical Quarterly* for 1946.

Some of Parker's ideas are well set forth in his speeches as a Congressman, in the *Congressional Globe*. The *Globe*, and its successor (the *Congressional Record*), and the published reports of Congressional committees contain much of value concerning the Indian Territory in Parker's day. The annual reports of the Commissioner of Indian Affairs are useful. Much more important, for the Fort Smith court, are the annual reports of the Attorney General. Here are statistics for all the district courts, detailed information concerning individual pardon applications, and special reports about deputy marshals, jail conditions and the like.

There is an excellent article on Parker in the *Chronicles of Oklahoma* for 1933. Written by a lawyer, Harry P. Dailey, this article stresses the appeals to the Supreme Court.

James O. Murphy studied the Parker court as part of his work for the master's degree. His thesis, which emphasizes appeals, court costs, changing jurisdiction, and so forth, is on file at the University of Oklahoma library. It has never been published.

There are two recent biographies of famous individuals who appeared before Parker: Burton Rascoe's *Belle Starr, "the Bandit Queen"*; and *Land Hunger: David L. Payne and the Oklahoma Boomers*, by C. C. Rister. The Rister book, based on painstaking research, is both dependable and entertaining. Rascoe's volume cannot be so highly recommended, for it contains many errors; but it does contain hitherto-unpublished materials and explodes some frontier myths.

Any one interested in the Indian Territory should read the many splendid books which have been turned out by Grant Foreman and Angie Debo. For the Parker story, Foreman's *History of Oklahoma* has the greatest value; but attention is also called to his *Muskogee, the Biography of an Oklahoma Town*. The Fort Smith court figures in several Debo volumes: *The Rise and Fall of the Choctaw Republic; The Road to Disappearance* (which deals with the Creeks); *And Still the Waters Run* (on the liquidation of the Five Civilized Tribes); and *Tulsa: from Creek Town to Oil Capital*.

Nor should the reader miss Morris L. Wardell's *Political History of the Cherokee Nation;* and E. E. Dale's *Cow Country;* and a personal account, *When the Daltons Rode*, by the famous Emmett Dalton. Zoe A. Tilghman's *Marshal of the Last Frontier* deals with Bill Tilghman, who captured Bill Doolin at

Eureka Springs. A new book of real merit is Wayne Gard's *Frontier Justice.*

On the Arkansas side, I may mention the state histories by D. Y. Thomas and D. T. Herndon; and John Gould Fletcher's recent book on Arkansas. J. Fred Patton has written a history of Fort Smith; but, sad to say, this has not appeared in book form. It was published in the Arkansas Centennial edition of the Fort Smith newspaper, the *Southwest American,* in 1936.

E. M. Borchard and E. R. Lutz give a chapter to a Parker case in their *Convicting the Innocent.* On the basis of the published pardon records, they claim that William Woods and Henry Miller should not have been found guilty in 1888. It may be said, however, that other accounts of the Woods-Miller trial show the matter in a somewhat different light.

I have left for last the most important book of all, one published in Fort Smith in 1898. This is S. W. Harman's *Hell on the Border; He Hanged Eighty-Eight Men. A History of the Great United States Criminal Court at Fort Smith, Arkansas, and of Crime and Criminals in the Indian Territory, and the Trial and Punishment thereof Before his Honor Judge Isaac C. Parker, "the Terror of Law-Breakers," and by the Courts of Said Territory, Embracing the Leading Sentences and Charges to Grand and Petit Juries Deliverd (sic) by the World Famous Jurist—His Acknowledged Masterpieces, Besides Much Other Legal Lore of Untold Value to Attorneys, and of Interest to Readers in Every Walk of Life—a Book for the Millions—Illustrated with over Fifty Fine Half Tones.*

198

Harman's book is as strange as its title. It offers inspirational poems by C. P. Sterns; warnings to the young; wholly untrue yarns about the border outlaws, whom Harman secretly admired; and a good deal of advertising for J. Warren Reed, a criminal lawyer who helped finance publication.

Still, *Hell on the Border* is an important book. It contains the personal reminiscences of Harman, who hung around the Fort Smith court during Parker's last years as judge, and was jury foreman at Cherokee Bill's second trial. Included also are some of the reminiscences of Lawyer Reed, and items culled from border newspapers now difficult to find. The book needs checking at every point, for it contains many direct misstatements. It overemphasizes the last third of Parker's years in Fort Smith—the period of Harman's residence in the border city. The statistical tables, compiled by Sterns, are not trustworthy. (As an example, Colorado Bill, who was hanged in 1879, is listed twice in the execution section, under different names.) But, for all its faults, *Hell on the Border* is a fascinating and indispensable book, a pioneer effort in the field.

Index

200

INDEX

201

INDEX

202

INDEX